LETTERS TO PALESTINE

LETTERS TO PALESTINE

Writers Respond to War and Occupation

Edited by Vijay Prashad
Foreword by Junot Díaz

VERSO

London • New York

First published by Verso Books 2015
The collection © Verso 2015
Contributions © Contributors 2015

The foreword by Junot Díaz comes from off-the-cuff remarks he made
at Clark University, Worcester, MA, on September 30, 2014.
The introduction by Vijay Prashad is based on his report
for *Red Pepper*, October/November 2014.
An earlier version of Ben Ehrenreich's essay was published
in the *Los Angeles Review of Books*.
Deema K. Shehabi's "Gate of Freedom" first appeared on the Academy of
American Poets website as the Poem of the Day on March 10, 2013.
An earlier version of Colin Dayan's essay was published in the *Boston Review*.
Nora Barrows-Friedman's essay is an edited excerpt from her new book, *In Our
Power: US Students Organize for Justice in Palestine* (Just World Books, 2014).

1 3 5 7 9 10 8 6 4 2

Verso
UK: 6 Meard Street, London W1F 0EG
US: 20 Jay Street, Suite 1010, Brooklyn, NY 11201
www.versobooks.com

Verso is the imprint of New Left Books

ISBN-13: 978-1-78478-067-8 (PB)
eISBN-13: 978-1-78478-259-7 (US)
eISBN-13: 978-1-78478-294-8 (UK)

British Library Cataloguing in Publication Data
A catalogue record for this book is available from the British Library

Library of Congress Cataloging-in-Publication Data
A catalog record for this book is available from the Library of Congress

Typeset in Electra by Hewer Text UK Ltd, Edinburgh, Scotland
Printed in the US by Maple Press

CONTENTS

War Reports

Politics

Foreword:
Americans Are So Deranged
About Palestine

Junot Díaz

I grew up in the '80s in Central New Jersey, and every single kind of colonial settler calamity was present in my community. I was friends with an Irish kid, the only white kid in our community, and a hard-core Irish Catholic republican. His family used to pass the hat around in church to raise money for the IRA. My other friend was an Egyptian kid whose family extended into Palestine, and throughout the '80s, while everybody else was watching John Hughes movies, this kid had me on point on Palestine. And then of course this was at the height of the apartheid movement. So all of my African American friends, well, two of them, not all of them, had parents who were part of the leftwing, pro-ANC, anti-apartheid movement. I'm in this poor community and this is all just getting beamed into my head.

So by the time I was in college, I could give you chapter and verse on anti-Zionist projects. And look, for many people it's a really tough issue. It's like we've kind of gotten deranged, so that there are certain areas we can't discuss. And of course the situation in Palestine is an utter taboo in this country. Our ideas of terrorism, our ideas of Arabs, are over saturated with the most negative, weirdly perverse racist ideologies. I can't even turn on the news for five seconds without hearing the most racist shit about Arabs or Muslims. And so in that kind of atmosphere, it's just a shouting match. If you say, I think the occupation of Palestine is fucked up on forty different levels, people are like, you're the devil, we're going to get your tenure taken away, we're going to destroy you. You can say almost anything else. You could be like, "I eat humans," and they'll be like *bien, bien.*

On the basic, basic level: If you are occupying other people's shit, guess what—you are fucked up. That's that. And that's a tough thing for people to stomach. Because we live in a country that's currently occupying people's fucking land. Perhaps Americans are so deranged about Palestine because Americans are thinking, if we give up here, these fucking Indians are going to want their shit back. Well, maybe they should get their shit back. Since 90 percent of us don't own anything, I don't know how much it would hurt us.

Introduction:
A Country in Darkness

Vijay Prashad

Forget Palestine

Palestine is easily forgotten. There is war. There is suffering. The war ends. The suffering vanishes. Silence.

Was there even a "war"? Palestine is under occupation, and has been since 1967, since 1948. An occupied land is not at war, can never be at war. It is occupied. Occupation is a state of war. The occupied space retaliates. It seeks its freedom. It is punished. Was Operation Protective Edge a war or a punishment? Operation Grapes of Wrath, Operation Cast Lead, Operation Pillar of Cloud—names less of defense and more of vengeful retribution.

On the night of Tuesday, July 29, 2014, three shells hit the Jabalia Elementary Girls School in Gaza—a UN-designated emergency shelter for 3,300 Palestinians. Those who had taken refuge there came because the Israelis had warned them to leave their homes. The UN had given the Israelis the coordinates of this school seventeen times. Their warnings made no impact. The shells killed at least sixteen people and wounded hundreds. The UN Relief and Works Agency for Palestinian Refugees (UNRWA) chief, Pierre Krähenbühl, said in a powerful statement, "Children killed in their sleep; this is an affront to all of us, a source of universal shame. Today, the world stands disgraced." Israel destroyed Gaza's only power plant, which impacted the already fragile sewage and water purification system as well as food storage. Electricity was mostly off, which meant that the Palestinians were cut off from the world. As it is, when Israel conducts its "operations" inside Gaza, it seals the area, preventing media from entrance. The aftermath of these operations has been devastating, whether in Gaza City's neighborhood of Shuja'iyya or the town of Khuza'a. Forty-four percent of Gaza's 140 square miles (360 square km) was designated a "buffer zone" by the Israelis. By the end of this pummeling Gaza's Ministry of Health puts the figure for the dead at over 2,000 and the wounded over 11,000. Seven of ten Palestinians killed in this war were children.

The UN Human Rights Council voted for an investigation of alleged war crimes by Israel against the Palestinians. The call for accountability came from most of the world's states. But accountability there will not be. Indeed, there is barely memory. Palestine is forgotten.

As I write these lines, Jerusalem is in torment. Tensions are about as high as they were in 2000—when Ariel Sharon went to the Al-Aqsa Mosque. I watch a video taken by B'Tselem of a disabled twelve-year-old boy, a-Rajbi, being detained by two strapping Israeli soldiers; they handcuff him brutally as he stands there and screams near his village of Jabel Johar, Hebron, near the settlement of Kiryat Arba. The settlers stand and cheer, one throwing out a clichéd racist slur. I watch another video of an Israeli officer accusing Israeli activists of treason for trying to prevent the removal of Palestinian farmers from their land. There are fast-moving tragedies. Already the 2014 Gaza War seems dwarfed by the escalation in Jerusalem.

One day Palestine will become what it wants. But that day is not now. Now Palestine is a shadow.

I drew her bleeding

One more war, one more exhausting period for the Palestinians filled with death and destruction, terror and its traumas. Wars come in a sequence: 2014, 2012, 2009, 2006 . . . This chain of numbers says nothing of the everyday war that eclipses the smiles of ordinary people who have to make bare lives in extraordinary times. Every document of the Israeli occupation and suffocation of Gaza resembles every other one. There are the forensic texts of human rights groups and the UN commissions—actuaries of the occupation, the authors of these documents give us the scaffolding of devastation. Poets and filmmakers, storytellers and pamphleteers fill their artifacts with sentiment. How many times can a human being hear that in seven weeks the Israelis killed over 2,000 people, injured tens of thousands, demolished the lives of hundreds of thousands, wiped out buildings that heal, teach and shelter?

Fida Qishta, born and raised in Rafah (Palestine), took her video camera around to document life in her Gaza. She put her story together in a painful meditation of a film, *Where Should the Birds Fly* (2012). Scenes of ordinary farmers and fisherfolk trying to ply their trade, while Israeli snipers and gunboats shoot at them, get straight to the point. All those who talk of Hamas rockets being fired into Israel should take a look at this section of Qishta's film, where there is a banal, even tendentious use of the gun to degrade and frighten unarmed Palestinians as they try to make a living. Bulldozers and border crossings make it impossible to lead lives. Then comes Cast Lead (2009). It is a good thing that Qishta has her camera and that she is so brave. The scenes are disturbing and honest—there is nothing manufactured about her film. We are there on the day (January 18) an Israeli attack killed forty-eight members of the family of Helmi and Maha Samouni, whose house in Zeitoun, in the suburbs of Gaza City, was bombed and then occupied. The departing Israeli soldiers left behind love notes to Palestine, graffiti in Hebrew and English: *Arabs need 2 die, Make War Not Peace, 1 is down, 999,999 to go, Arabs 1948–2009.* Qishta went to see fifteen-year-old Ayman al-Najar, victim of an Israeli bomb which killed his sister, in Nasser

Hospital in Khan Yunis. He shows Qishta his wounds, his body wracked by white phosphorus burns (the graphic image sears). Qishta takes refuge at a UN compound, a shelter to fleeing Palestinian families. Israeli F-16s release their bombs; some land on the UN buildings, the night resplendent with the white phosphorus traces, beautiful in the sky, barbaric on the skin.

Then we meet Mona. She is the highlight of this disturbingly accurate film. At age ten, she is Qishta's guide into the suffering and resilience of Gaza. Her farming family were herded into a neighbors' home by Israeli troops who accuse her brother of being with Hamas; the home is then bombed from the sky. Qishta asks Mona how many people in her family died that day. "In my immediate family?" asks Mona, innocent to the gravity of her own question. So much death, but she appears resigned and wise. "If we die," she says gravely, "we die. If we survive, we survive." She shows Qishta a drawing she did of the massacre. "It was a sea of blood and body parts," she says. "They took the most precious beloved of my heart," meaning her parents. She points to a person in her drawing, "This is Palestine. I drew her bleeding."

Watching Qishta's film once more during this current war brings out all the clichés of Israeli violence—the same excuses, the same brutal attack on civilians, the same paralysis on the ground. What was 2009 could have been 2014. It is all one period, punctuated by moments of anticipation.

Hamas

From its emergence in May 1964 to its exile from Beirut in August 1982, the Palestinian Liberation Organization was the main—and in many ways only—resistance organization of the Palestinian people. The PLO and its leader Yasser Arafat picked up the mantle of anticolonialism and national liberation movements in the 1960s to good effect. Algeria, Vietnam, Palestine—to have linked the Palestinian struggle to the Algerian and the Vietnamese wars of liberation was a major accomplishment of Yasser Arafat's PLO. But the Israeli and Jordanian assault on it in Jordan in 1970 and then the Israeli invasion of Beirut in 1982 crushed its capacity to act in the area close to Israel. Even in Tunisia, the PLO was not safe. Israel's fighter jets bombed the PLO headquarters in Tunis during Operation Wooden Leg in 1985, killing over eighty people. When the First Intifada broke out in the Occupied Territories in 1989, the PLO's links to the Palestinians in the camps and in the Occupied Territories had been weak. Others had grown to replace them. In Gaza, the most important movement that supplanted the PLO was Hamas, the Muslim Brotherhood's Palestinian organization. Gaza was under Israeli occupation and yet the Israelis allowed this movement— formed in 1988—to thrive. In 2009, an Israeli official told Andrew Higgins of the *Wall Street Journal*,

> Israel's military-led administration in Gaza looked favorably on the paraplegic cleric [Sheikh Yassin], who set up a wide network of schools, clinics, a library and kindergartens. Sheikh Yassin formed the Islamist group Mujama al-Islamiya, which was officially recognized by Israel as a charity and then, in 1979, as an association. Israel also endorsed the establishment of the Islamic University of Gaza, which it now regards as a hotbed of militancy. The university was one of the first targets hit by Israeli warplanes in the [2008–09 Operation Cast Lead].

Israel saw Mujama al-Islamiya, which would become Ḥarakat al-Muqāwamah al-ʾIslāmiyyah (Hamas: Islamic Resistance Movement), as the lesser of two evils. The real problem for Israel was the secular PLO. It had to be crushed. But the PLO, in exile and cut off from the Palestinian people, hastened to make any kind of deal to allow its leadership access to its land. The Oslo accords of 1994 must be seen in that context. But even Oslo, the surrender of the Palestinian leadership, was not enough for Israel. During the Second Intifada, the Israelis decided to destroy Arafat. In fact, on December 3, 2001, at a cabinet meeting, Ariel Sharon said, "Arafat is no longer relevant." What was relevant was not Arafat himself but the image of Palestinian resistance. A desperate Arafat said on December 16 that attacks on Israelis must end, and so his

PLO fighters clashed with Hamas to stop them from their attacks. But this was not enough for the Israelis. The Israeli army's Chief of Staff Shaul Mofaz said that the PLO crackdown on Hamas was insufficient. The Palestinian Authority, he said, "is infected by terror from head to toe and does everything to disrupt our lives and to bring terrorism to our doorstep." The hammer came down heavily on the PLO. The life of resistance was to be knocked out of it.

At this time, the Israelis also turned their gunsights on Hamas. In January 2004, Sheikh Yassin said he was willing to end armed resistance against Israel if a Palestinian state was created in the West Bank, Gaza and east Jerusalem. Hamas's political leader Abdel Aziz al-Rantissi also concurred, saying that the Palestinians would declare a decade long *hudna* in exchange for independence. On March 22, Israel assassinated Sheikh Yassin. Two hundred thousand people attended his funeral. On April 17, they killed al-Rantissi. Any talk by Hamas of peace was met with assassination.

Hamas is one of the vehicles for Palestinian national aspirations. It is not necessarily the vehicle preferred by many Palestinians. There are many Palestinian Christians and nationalists, non–Muslim Brothers and communists who would like to have a different vehicle for their ambitions. But the Israelis have tethered the PLO through the Oslo process, destroyed the left outfits through assassination and incarceration. Israel asks, where is the secular and nonviolent Palestinian movement? It is sitting in Israel's prisons. What it allows to live is Hamas, and then it says that the Palestinians choose Hamas, and then Israel says that the Palestinians force Israel to violence . . .

Resistance

Palestine lies on its rickety bed. Israel stands above, pillow in hand. It places it on the face of Palestine. Palestine struggles. It pushes back. In the next bed sits Egypt. It is silent. Its pockets are filled with US dollars, handed over in exchange for a signature at Camp David. Jordan is on the floor. It looks sad, shaken. It does nothing. Nearby the King of Saudi

Arabia seems to be speaking about war crimes, sucking his oxygen container in jerks, wondering why it is taking so long for Israel to vanquish his enemies inside Palestine—Hamas, the Muslim Brotherhood's Palestinian wing. No one comes to Palestine's aid. The UN is in the corner. It has been banished by the United States, who stands close by, with its two mouths saying two different things. Palestine struggles alone.

Israel turns, hand on the pillow, pushing down, and says, look—look, Palestine is threatening us, endangering our lives. Others look away, giving Israel license to push harder.

The doctrine of self-defense does not apply to Palestine. It must take the pillow on its face willingly and allow itself to be asphyxiated. Resistance is a doctrine afforded to all, but denied to Palestine.

What is Palestine to do? It fires rockets. These are miserable devices. They fly erratically and scare their adversaries, but kill very few, destroy very little. Why, ask the liberal detractors, do they bother with these rockets? After all, they do no damage and they allow Israel justification for its violence.

What is Palestine to do? Not fire rockets? Conduct a mass civil disobedience campaign? Ah, yes. A good idea, drawing from Gandhi and Mandela—a massive march from Ramallah to Gaza that comes up against the Israeli separation walls and the Israeli forces—making their political leaders decide if they can simply fire on thousands of unarmed Palestinians who want to part the Israeli landscape to join their bifurcated lands.

Sitting in the darkness of Israel's Hadarim Prison is one of Palestine's most important political figures, Marwan Barghouti. He has been a guest of Israeli incarceration since 2002—on charges, unproven, that he is a terrorist. For the past decade, Barghouti has called for a general political resistance to Israel, earning him—as he sits in solitary confinement—the title "Palestine's Mandela." Why does Israel hold people like Marwan Barghouti in its cells? Why does Israel arrest all those who want a serious political dialogue and who are able to carry mass support, including those who favor a civil disobedience strategy? Here is where Israel wants the conversation to disappear. It is enough to say, "but Hamas is firing rockets and so we have to retaliate." It does not want to talk about other strategies. These would not allow it to perpetuate its policy of annexation through settlements (in the West Bank and East Jerusalem) and through the production of misery (in Gaza).

Israel planned to build settlements on a pocket of land just east of Jerusalem called E1. For two nights in January 2013, 300 activists set up camp there. They called their village Bab al-Shams, the gate of the sun. The name comes from the novel by Elias Khoury, *Bab al-Shams* (1998), which tells the story of a Palestinian couple, Younis and Nahila, one a fighter in Lebanon and the other a defender of their home in the Galilee. The couple meets secretly in a cave called Bab al-Shams, their haven. The activists who created their village of Bab al-Shams called it their "gate to our freedom and steadfastness." They had no rockets, no weapons. The young activists came out of the popular resistance committees. Their politics reflected their frustration with the strategy of negotiation and conciliation. "For decades," said the organizers of the village, "Israel has established facts on the ground as the international community has remained silent in response to these violations. The time has come to change the rules of the game, for us to establish facts on the ground—our own land."

The day after their encampment was first put up, Elias Khoury sent the citizens of Bab al-Shams a letter. "I see in your village all the faces of the loved ones who departed on the way to the land of our Palestinian promise," he wrote. "Palestine is the promise of the strangers who were expelled from their land and continue to be expelled every day from their homes. I see in your eyes a nation born from the rubble of the Nakba that has gone on for sixty-four years. I see you and in my heart the words grow. I see the words and you grow in my heart, rise high and burst into the sky." Israel destroyed the camp three times, even though the activists had broken no Israeli law (they used tents, which did not require permits). The activists kept rebuilding their camp until Israeli Prime Minister Benjamin Netanyahu ordered that the area be designated as a closed military zone. The pillow had to remain on the face of Palestine.

Palestine, pillow on its face, has to defend the rockets that get fired out of its tattered body; Israel, pushing the pillow down, has never been called to account for its incarceration of Palestine's most serious and popular political leaders.

Sitting in his prison, during this Gaza war, Barghouti said, "Resistance as an option is and will remain a sufficient method for retaining freedom and independence." If Palestine does not resist, it will be fully suffocated—no way to breathe, no dignity.

Investigation

Ceasefires have come and gone before. They promise little. The basic facts of the situation do not change. There is no move to lift the suffocation of Palestine—to end the embargo on Gaza, to allow the Palestinians to form their own state, to agree to borders (Israel does not have declared borders, and yet demands that *it* be recognized—how can Palestine formally recognize a country whose borders are not clear?). None of this has happened.

Eternal return is the sensibility of these conflicts—no forward motion.

The one proposal that affords some international consensus is for the United Nations to investigate the nature of the conflict, to ensure that that allegations of war crimes heard by the UN Human Rights Council should be fully looked into. The Council's vote to set up a body for an investigation needs to be fully implemented. Israel has already closed the door to the investigators from Amnesty International and Human Rights Watch. In 2009, Israel prevented a previous UN panel from studying the nature of Operation Cast Lead—its investigation of people inside Israel had to be done over the telephone. A UN member state so cavalierly snubs a UN agency with an overwhelming mandate to do its job. Will the UN at least be able to undertake a proper investigation of the attacks on its institutions by Israel's armed forces? Without being able to interview those troops and study their target information, any investigation would be incomplete. Israel will contend that the attacks were carried out in error, or else that the targets were not UN buildings at the time but launch pads for Hamas. Israel is going to block any serious investigation of war crimes.

Even with an investigation, nothing will come of it. The Goldstone Report on the 2009 war had sufficient information to indict many Israeli leaders for war crimes, and yet no process was taken forward. On behalf of Israel, the US lobbied hard to prevent any discussion of the Goldstone Report in the appropriate UN forums. In 2009, then US Ambassador to the UN Susan Rice told UN Secretary General Ban Ki-moon several times to stop the progress of an inquiry. She told International Criminal Court President Sang-Hyun Song to block any move to consider Israeli actions against Palestine. "How the ICC handles issues concerning the Goldstone Report will be perceived by many in the US as a test for the ICC, as this is a very sensitive matter." In other words, if the ICC went ahead with the Report the US would consider freezing out the institution. It was a direct threat.

During the current ceasefire talks in Cairo, Israel insisted that the Palestinians concede that they should demand no investigation of the nature of the war and no accountability. It was a remarkable negotiating point. One thought was that Hamas would also be pulled up for war crimes, and so would be uneasy with a UN investigation. Izzat al-Rishq, a Hamas politburo member, said he was not bothered about this aspect. He said that the Palestinians should "act as soon as possible." Israel has already begun to discredit the UN Human Rights Council's investigation committee, calling its members "anti-Israel," while its UN Ambassador Ron Prosor tried to deflect attention by calling for an investigation of Hamas' rockets. Netanyahu defined the Israeli response to an investigation: "The report of this committee has already been written. The committee chairman has already decided that Hamas is not a terrorist organization. Therefore, they have nothing to look for here. They should visit Damascus, Baghdad and Tripoli. They should go see ISIS, the Syrian army and Hamas. There they will find war crimes, not here." On November 12, 2014, the Israeli Foreign Ministry informed the United Nations that it would not cooperate with the UN investigation. Palestine, meanwhile, joined the ICC in early 2015. Israel threatened to retaliate with a more aggressive settlement policy. The United States threatened to cut its modest humanitarian aid to Ramallah.

Solidarity

No country is as complicit in Israel's occupation and wars as the United States. It provides the diplomatic and military support that Israel needs to continue to garrison the Palestinians, make their lives more difficult and migration more appealing. The general tenor of US political fealty to Israeli policy was laid out by US President Gerald Ford to Israeli Prime Minister Yitzhak Rabin in 1975: "Should the US desire in the future to put forward proposals of its own, it will make every effort to coordinate with Israel its proposals with a view to refraining from putting forth proposals that Israel would consider unsatisfactory." The US government recognizes that while it will plead the Israeli case, it cannot be seen as doing nothing for the Palestinians. Richard Nixon told his consigliere Henry Kissinger in 1973, "You've got to give [the Palestinians] hope. It's really a—frankly, let's face it; you've got to make them think that there's some motion; that something is going on; that we're really doing our best with the Israelis." This dance has been going on from Nixon and Golda Meir to Barack Obama and Benjamin Netanyahu, and will likely continue. The fraudulent "peace process," maintained with complete cynicism by the United States, has smothered Palestinian dreams.

Slowly, cautiously, sections of the US population have broken with the pro-Israel consensus. Solidarity with Palestine has been a consistent feature of the US left. The brave young activists who founded the International Solidarity Movement (ISM) in 2001 brought their bodies to bear against the Israeli military's expansionist policies. Israeli bulldozers and bullets took the lives of young ISM volunteers Rachel Corrie and Tom Hurndall. This was courageous work, the province of a small number of hardened activists. Four years later, in 2005, activists from Palestine's growing civil society organizations formed the Boycott, Divestment and Sanctions (BDS) movement. BDS called upon people of good conscience to abjure any cooperation—both direct and indirect—with institutions and firms that participate in the occupation of Palestine. BDS asks less in terms of solidarity—one does not have to risk one's own body before a bulldozer or bullet; nonetheless, the backlash against the movement has been fierce. BDS provided an avenue for mass political participation, drawing large numbers of people into concrete action to put pressure on Israel. The BDS movement has grown exponentially across the world, including in the United States. It is a movement designed for international solidarity.

Not far from the offices of Palestine civil society organizations are the prisons that house some of Palestine's most distinguished political figures. The year after the BDS call was published, prisoners from different factions (the Democratic Front for the Liberation of Palestine, Fatah, Hamas, Islamic Jihad, and the Popular Front for the Liberation of Palestine) produced a National Reconciliation Document. This "Prisoners' Document" called for unity among all organized political forces to rekindle a national liberation movement for Palestine. If BDS invited the world to stand against Israel, the Prisoners' Document called upon Palestine to stand up for itself. These are the two sides of solidarity. BDS and the Prisoners' Document are the two inextricable pillars for solidarity with Palestine.

Documents

This is a book of documents. They are whispers from corners of the United States of America, whose government has been Israel's great enabler. The authors of these documents are committed to the people of Palestine as much as to humanity. These are writers who have taken positions, who have traveled to the occupied zones and written diaries, who have modulated their screams into poems and who have conjured up strategies for the streets, the boardrooms, and across the centers of political life. These writers are people that I greatly admire. That they would take the time to so hastily produce such beautiful work to fight against the amnesia over Gaza and the disavowal of Palestinian politics is itself an indication of the worlds that we are prepared to fight against and the worlds we would like to create. These cultural offerings are bundled into this book for Palestine. These are our letters. Please deliver them to the present so that we can make a better future.

CONDITIONS

What Is Palestine to the US?

Mumia Abu-Jamal

For some, this may come as a surprise, for it seems illogical, but the US doesn't hate Palestine.

It arms and finances its nemesis, Israel—yes.

It votes consistently with Israel in the United Nations—even against the majority of the world's nations—yes.

It quietly and surreptitiously allowed Israel to become a nuclear power—yes.

All this is true; but the US doesn't hate Palestine. The truth is something far worse, for dismissal is more damning than hatred.

Palestine, its people, its history, its culture, its art, its poetry, its very land, is dismissed as a mere trifle by the US Empire, not dissimilar to the response of the old British Empire, which dispatched the lands, hopes and dreams of the Palestinians, with cold, imperial aplomb.

For empire is ever an exercise of global violence, for domination is but utter violation: the very root of violence.

It violates the human soul, which yearns for freedom.

Palestine was relegated to the misery of a warren of Middle Eastern ghettos for one reason—and one reason only.

To allow the erection of a colonial outpost from which Britain (and later the US) could exercise power in a region that held the greatest prize in world history: petroleum.

That outpost? Fortress Israel.

Petroleum lit the lampposts of London, and fueled the factories of America, leading to its Industrial Age.

It needed a sentry to protect this precious resource.

It needed a watchdog in this neighborhood.

Enter Fortress Israel.

Palestine is a minor afterthought to the US Empire and its imperialist apologists. Its pain, its sufferings, its gross humiliations don't bother the empire one whit.

Yet, to millions of people, throughout Europe, Africa, Asia, and the Americas, their unjust and cruel treatment at the hands of the Zionists finds purchase in hearts worldwide.

From their epic losses spring the fruits of a solidarity that binds us, human to human, oppressed to oppressed.

As the cruelties of imperialism mount, giving rise to anger and distaste, the forces of solidarity grow too, encapsulating the majority of the people of the Earth.

Bad Laws

Teju Cole

Not all violence is hot. There's cold violence too, which takes its time and finally gets its way. Children going to school and coming home are exposed to it. Fathers and mothers listen to politicians on television calling for their extermination. Grandmothers have no expectation that even their aged bodies are safe: Any young man may lay a hand on them with no consequence. The police could arrive at night and drag the family out into the street. Putting a people into deep uncertainty about the fundamentals of life, over years and decades, is a form of cold violence. Through an accumulation of laws rather than by military means, a particular misery is intensified and entrenched. This slow violence, this cold violence, no less than the other kind, ought to be looked at and understood.

Near the slopes of Mount Scopus in East Jerusalem is the neighborhood of Sheikh Jarrah. Most of the people who live here are Palestinian Arabs, and the area itself has an ancient history that features both Jews and Arabs.

The Palestinians of East Jerusalem are in a special legal category under modern Israeli law. Most of them are not Israeli citizens, nor are they classified the same way as people in Gaza or the West Bank. They are permanent residents. There are old Palestinian families here, but in a neighborhood like Sheikh Jarrah, many of the people are refugees who were settled here after the Catastrophe of 1948. They left their original homes behind, fleeing places like Haifa and Sarafand al-Amar, and they came to Sheikh Jarrah, which then became their home. Many of them were given houses constructed on a previously uninhabited parcel of land by the Jordanian government and by the UN Relief and Works Agency. East Jerusalem came under Israeli control in 1967, and since then, but with a greater tempo in recent years, these families are being rendered homeless a second or third time.

There are many things about Palestine that are not easily seen from a distance. The beauty of the land, for instance, is not at all obvious. Scripture and travelers' reports describe a harsh terrain of stone and rocks, a place in which it is difficult to find water or shelter from the sun. Why would anyone want this land? But then you visit and you understand the attenuated intensity of what you see. You get the sense that there are no wasted gestures, that this is an economical landscape, and that there is great beauty in this economy. The sky is full of clouds that are like flecks of white paint. The olive trees, the leaves of which have silvered undersides, are like an apparition. And even the stones and rocks speak of history, of deep time, and of the consolation that comes with all old places. This is a land of tombs, mountains, and mysterious valleys. All this one can only really see at close range.

Another thing one sees, obscured by distance but vivid up close, is that the Israeli oppression of Palestinian people is not as crude as Western media can make it seem. It is in fact an extremely refined process, one that involves a dizzying assemblage of laws and bylaws, contracts, ancient documents, force, amendments, customs, religion, conventions, and sudden irrational moves, all of this mixed together and imposed with the greatest care.

The impression this insistence on legality confers, from the Israeli side, is of an infinitely patient due process that will eventually pacify the enemy and guarantee security. The reality, from the Palestinian side, is of a suffocating viciousness. The fate of Palestinian Arabs since the Catastrophe has been to be scattered and oppressed by different means: in the West Bank, in Gaza, inside the 1948 borders, in Jerusalem, in refugee camps abroad, in Jordan, in the distant diaspora. In all these places, Palestinians experience restrictions on their freedom and on their movement. To be Palestinian is to be hemmed in. Much of this is done by brute military force from the IDF—mass killing for which no later accounting is possible—or on an individual basis in the secret chambers of the Shin Bet; but a lot of it is done according to Israeli law, argued in and approved by Israeli courts, and technically legal, even when the laws in question are bad laws and in clear contravention of international standards and conventions.

The reality is that, as a Palestinian Arab, in order to defend yourself against the persecution you face, not only do you have to be an expert in Israeli law, you also have to be a Jewish Israeli and have the force of the Israeli state as your guarantor. You have to be what you are not, what it is not possible for you to be, in order not to be slowly strangled by the laws arrayed against you. In Israel, there is no pretense that the opposing parties in these cases are equal before the law; or, rather, such a pretense exists, but no one on either side takes it seriously. This has certainly been the reality for the Palestinian families living in Sheikh Jarrah whose homes, built mostly in 1956, inhabited by three or four generations of people, are being taken from them by legal means.

As in other neighborhoods in East Jerusalem—Har Homa, the Old City, Mount Scopus, Jaffa Gate—there is a policy at work in Sheikh Jarrah. This policy is twofold. The first is the systematic removal of Palestinian Arabs, either by banishing individuals on the basis of paperwork, or by taking over or destroying their homes by court order. Thousands of people have had their residency revoked on a variety of flimsy pretexts: time spent living abroad, time spent living elsewhere in Occupied Palestine, and so on. The permanent residency of a Palestinian in East Jerusalem is anything but permanent, and once it is revoked, is almost impossible to recover.

The second aspect of the policy is the systematic increase of the Jewish populations of these neighborhoods. This latter goal is driven both by national and municipal legislation (under the official rubric of "demographic balance") and is sponsored in part by wealthy Zionist activists who, unlike their defenders in the Western world, are proud to embrace the word "Zionist." However, it is not the wealthy Zionists who move into these homes or claim these lands: It is ideologically and religiously extreme Israeli Jews, some of whom are poor Jewish immigrants to the state of Israel. And when they move in—when they raise the Israeli flag over a house that, until yesterday, was someone else's ancestral home, or when they begin new constructions on the rubble of other people's homes—they act as anyone would who was above the law: callously, unfeelingly, unconcerned about the humiliation of their neighbors. This twofold policy, of pushing out Palestinian Arabs and filling the land with Israeli Jews, is recognized by all the parties involved. And for such a policy, the term "ethnic cleansing" is not too strong: It is in fact the only accurate description.

Each Palestinian family that is evicted in Sheikh Jarrah is evicted for different reasons. But the fundamental principle at work is usually similar: An activist Jewish organization makes a claim that the land on which the house was built was in Jewish hands before 1948. There is sometimes paperwork that supports this claim (there is a lot of citation of nineteenth-century Ottoman Land Law), and sometimes the paperwork is forged, but the court will hear and, through eccentric interpretations of these old laws, often agree to the claim. The violence this legality contains is precisely that no Israeli court will hear a corresponding claim from a Palestinian family. What Israeli law supports, de facto, is the right of return for Jews into East Jerusalem. What it cannot countenance is the right of return of Palestinians into the innumerable towns, villages, and neighborhoods all over Palestine, from which war, violence, and law have expelled them.

History moves at great speed, as does politics, and Zionists understand this. The pressure to continue the ethnic cleansing of East Jerusalem is already met with pressure from the other side to stop this clear violation of international norms. And so, Zionist lawyers and lawmakers move with corresponding speed, making new laws, pushing through new interpretations, all in order to ethnically cleanse the land of Palestinian presence. And though Palestinians make their own case, long and loud, and even though they persist in the face of despair—and though many young Jews, beginning to wake up to the crimes of their nation, have marched in support of the families evicted or under threat in Sheikh Jarrah—the law and its innovative interpretations evolve at a speed that makes self-defense all but impossible.

This cannot go on. The example of Sheikh Jarrah, the cold violence of it, is echoed all over Palestine. Side by side with this cold violence is, of course, the hot violence that dominates the news: Israel's periodic wars on Gaza, its blockades on places like Nablus, the random unanswerable acts of murder in places like Hebron. In no sane future of humanity should the deaths of hundreds of children continue to be accounted collateral damage, as Israel did in the summer of 2014.

In the world's assessment of the situation in Palestine, in coming to understand why the Palestinian situation is urgent, the viciousness of law must be taken as seriously as the cruelties of war. As in other instances in which world opinion forced a large-scale systemic oppression to come to an end, we must begin by calling things by their proper names. Israel uses an extremely complex legal and bureaucratic apparatus to dispossess Palestinians of their land, hoping perhaps to forestall accusations of a brutal land grab. No one is fooled by any of this. Nor is anyone fooled by the accusation, common to many of Israel's defenders, that any criticism of Israeli policies amounts to anti-Semitism. The historical suffering of Jewish people is real, but it is no less real than, and does not in any way justify, the present oppression of Palestinians by Israeli Jews.

A neighborhood like Sheikh Jarrah is an X-ray of Israel at the present moment: a limited view showing a single set of features, but significant to the entire body politic. The case that is being made, and that must continue to be made to all people of conscience, is that Israel's occupation of Palestine is criminal. This case should also include the argument that the proliferation of bad laws by the legislature and courts of Israel is itself anti-Semitic, and that these laws constitute a grave offence to the dignity of both Jews and Palestinians.

Travel Diary

Noura Erakat

In late May 2013, I co-led an Interfaith Peace Builders (IFPB) delegation to Israel and the Occupied West Bank, including East Jerusalem, along with Josh Ruebner, author and national advocacy director of the US Campaign to End the Israeli Occupation. Though we reached the edge of Gaza, we could not enter due to Israel's hermetic seal of the 360-square mile Strip. Over the span of two weeks available we sought to explore the impact of US foreign policy upon the Israel-Palestinian conflict. We traveled from the Jordan Valley to Lifta; from Jerusalem and through the cow-herding stalls of the Qalandia checkpoint; from Dheisheh refugee camp to surrounding, and enduring, Bethlehem; from the heart of Nazareth to the colony that sits on its highest points; from the ignominious parks of south Tel Aviv to the gentrified shores of Jaffa; from the resilient communities of Bil'in and Nahalin to the tortured streets of Hebron where militarized racial supremacy is painfully raw.

Throughout the trip, the delegates examined how they, through US economic, military, and diplomatic aid, were complicit in this seemingly distant conflict. This was no exercise in Western voyeurism. In the course of paying taxes and letting elected representatives rattle off their allegiance to Israel without scrutiny, each of the delegates was both part of the problem and a key to its resolution. This is what Josh and I repeatedly emphasized.

In the course of co-leading the delegation, I had to contend with my own personal challenge. As much as I had worked, studied, and lived in the region, my American privilege had afforded a comfortable distance to speak as an advocate and scrutinize as a scholar. That convenient distance was swiftly dashed before arrival. Anticipating, as always, the reality of being denied entry, I traveled through the Allenby crossing. The rest of the delegates entered through the Tel Aviv airport. At the close of our second day, my interventions moved from the historical, the legal, and the political, to the familial, to loss, and to the fragility of futures. I preferred "objectivity" and its promised comfort but I could not escape biography and experience.

I struggled with the question of whether or not to publish this diary. Aside from the vulnerability that it reveals, it embodies a voice with which I have not spoken in for many years. In a challenging exchange with two of my dearest friends and colleagues, I explained that the writing, and the trip more generally, felt like a regression to a place I had once been. To the beginning of my journey as an activist; to the first delegation I led to the region at age nineteen when I worked with Global Exchange; to the first stories I listened to and shared during my time at Dheisheh refugee camp as an English instructor and later as a student at Hebrew University when the Second Intifada began. Then, as now, my reflections were raw. Their emotive thrust describes the resilience of survival and the violence of unrestrained state power at the expense of a more nuanced narrative and a more analytical inquiry. In doing so, I inadvertently created binaries of good and bad, victim and oppressor, helplessness and empowerment, thereby sacrificing the layered contradictions within spaces/societies in addition to the obvious ones between them.

One of my friends pointed out, for example, that I failed to mention even once the Palestinian Authority, its complicity in the occupation, and the associated networks of political and business elites who benefit from Oslo. He pointed out that my description of Palestinians seemed to romanticize them as a singular unit. It's true. Reading my essay, I was struck by how naive I sound in regard to Palestinians. I omitted my reaction to the socioeconomic stratification plainly evident in the largest Palestinian cities. Some Palestinians are doing quite well and have developed a vested interest in perpetuating the peace process industry. Others, mostly youth, could care less about the Palestinian question and seek prosperity and a semblance of normalcy in their daily lives. Nor did I reflect on how NGOs have supplanted liberation politics in Palestinian society and how this has stunted more vibrant mass movements.

I did not discuss my indignation when one of our *Palestinian* speakers refused to look me in the eye when he shook my hand to say goodbye; intuitively, I thought he disapproved of my exposed hair. I refrained from discussing the internalized racism that afflicts colonized societies. In particular, I did not share my encounter with a beautiful six-year-old girl who hoped to become more fair-skinned when she grew up. Her mother enthusiastically pointed to me and told her daughter, "See, she is dark-skinned and is an attorney. Tomorrow you will become a great doctor." In Hebron, I was annoyed by the tone of one of the Palestinian speakers. It was bombastic and sounded much more like a speech at a mass rally than a discussion with a sympathetic audience. Rather than reflect on it in my diary, I made excuses for him as he spoke. I left out my awkward experience in Sheikh Jarrah when Umm al-Kurd said in Arabic, "Americans do not like Jews and that's why they send them to us." As the only Arabic and English speaker at that moment, I hesitated to translate what she said for fear of exposing her to criticism. After thirty seconds of silence, I translated her words verbatim for the sake of integrity. My diary did not capture any of this nuance.

My other friend and reader, who possesses a close knowledge of Israeli society, was struck by my two-dimensional description of Israelis. She knows I know better, so what is going on, she asked. She too is right. I did not discuss our meetings with the Boycott From Within movement whose Israeli civil society leadership explicitly support BDS campaigns despite the high personal costs they incur. I did not

mention our meeting with New Profile leaders who seek to demilita-
rize Israeli society not just because of state violence meted against
Palestinians but also because of the destructive and formative impact
of militarization on young Israeli men and women. I did not explain
that a representative of Zochrot, an Israeli organization dedicated to
raising awareness about Israel's ethnic cleansing project within Israeli
society, guided us on our walk through Lifta. I did not reflect on the
young Israeli activist who has dedicated himself to achieving dignity
for the African refugees now stranded in Levinsky Park, who explained
that he fears traveling to the West Bank because of the danger posed by
Israeli soldiers.

Certainly none of these encounters demonstrates the existence of a
vibrant Israeli left or a formidable opposition movement. To the
contrary, most contemporary polls of Israelis show acceptance and
approval of an explicit Israeli apartheid model. Despite the ability to
vote freely, only a few thousand Israelis, if that, vote for Arab Israeli
political parties that strive for meaningful equality. Nonetheless, the
omission of these meetings reifies an ethno-racial "us versus them"
framework that I unintentionally constructed.

Even after editing the original diary, the one before you now, I remain
uneasy. It does not do justice to the layers of violence, historical depth,
and struggles within each of these local encounters. It is simply personal.
However, because of my conviction in the justness of the Palestinian
struggle for self-determination, freedom, and dignity, I fear that the
personal might appear unfair and even manipulative. Absent these binaries and rife with the complexity it deserves, I believe the justness of the
cause would be just as piercing. Israeli settler colonialism, apartheid,
and occupation should not cease because Palestinians are good and
Israelis are bad. Those structural conditions are an anathema to all
whom they directly and indirectly impact—whether they happen to
manifest across historic Palestine or elsewhere.

Day one (Jerusalem)

All thirty-three members of the Interfaith Peace Builders delegation have arrived. Not an ordinary feat in light of routine practice by Israel to restrict entry to travelers empathetic to Palestinians, including such globally renowned travelers like Noam Chomsky. Israel's primary targets of this policy are diasporic Palestinians themselves. They represent an achievement and a threat: an achievement because they have successfully been stripped of positive claims to be present and a threat because their return would disrupt Israel's socially constructed demographic majority. To avoid complications for the rest of the delegation, and as a Palestinian in diaspora, I traveled through the Allenby crossing by bus while the rest of the delegation traveled directly to Ben Gurion Airport.

Day two (Jerusalem)

We covered Jerusalem today. We studied retroactive taxes, denial of housing permits, and "center of life" fire hoops—a euphemism for the Israeli policy established in 1995 and applied only to Jerusalem's Palestinian population. It required that Palestinians demonstrate that Jerusalem has been their continuous place of residence for seven years. Failure to do so results in the revocation of their residency permits. The center of life laws are among the cold and toxic maneuvers of Israeli bureaucracy that pluck out Palestinians one by one. It was a fierce study in just how "blind" the law is.

Like Chinese torture, compulsion here does not require dramatic fanfare. The administrative measures are an interminable march toward hegemony. They lack the drama of forced evictions but produce the same results in the name of administrative coherence. The state has revoked 14,000 residency permits from Palestinians throughout the West Bank since 1967 and counting. It has destroyed 26,000 homes belonging to Palestinians to date.

In some instances the ethnic cleansing is outright brutal: building the Wall through homes, lands, lives; residency permit revocation; and settler takeovers. Rifqa al-Kurd (Umm al-Kurd) is ninety-two years old and originally from Haifa. She has been living in Sheikh Jarrah, an East Jerusalem suburb, since 1956. Sheikh Jarrah, along with Beit Safafa, Issawiya, Shu'fat, Silwan, and Beit Hanina, are all Palestinian suburbs of East Jerusalem that stand in the way of Israel's master plan to Judaize the city. According to the Jerusalem 2000 Plan, Israel aims to change the ratio of Christian and Muslim Palestinians and Jewish Israelis from a balance of 40 to 60 percent to one of 30 to 70 by 2020. To do so, the state is building two national parks, an eastern ring road, and several other national environmental projects where residents cannot live, Palestinian residents anyway. It is only a matter of time before the Israeli state designates them suitable for Jewish neighborhoods.

While the state has used a web of administrative practices to remove the inconveniently present Palestinian families, it has exerted no such niceties upon the residents of Sheikh Jarrah. There, the state's police forces have accompanied Jewish Israeli settlers and facilitated their takeover of Palestinian homes. Young settlers driven by a messianic calling have evicted Palestinians from their homes, settled in their place, and received adulation rather than contempt from Israel's rule of law machinations. A group of such settler boys have taken over part of Umm al-Kurd's home, which she built for her son and his family. He and his family now live elsewhere and visit their home occasionally. Daily, these settlers harass the matriarch; they release their dog onto her, her daughters, and her grandchildren; they taunt her that her days in her own home are numbered. In response, she tells the thirty-three American delegates that she will die in her home.

Day three (Ramallah)

The delegation spent a day in Ramallah, the most lively, dynamic, and vibrant Palestinian Bantustan. Here, the delegates met with representatives of Palestinian civil society, human rights organizations, and a highly educated intelligentsia: Addameer, Al Haq, the Boycott National Committee, and Palestinians With Dignity. The representatives spoke with piercing clarity and precision, and provided vision and hope to resist the pounding arm of steady ethnic cleansing. Most of their work is concentrated in Ramallah because they cannot get around the Occupied Palestinian Territories easily. It is also in Ramallah because it is geared toward moving an agenda on the international terrain.

To the dismay of a Palestinian national body, frustrated with the counterproductive effects of Oslo, none of the approaches are perfect and none are constitutive of a coherent Palestinian national liberation project, which does not exist at this time. Still, each is critical and indispensable.

The need to resist is as urgent as ever. I can travel freely precisely because the state registers me as American and not Palestinian. I can travel along roads, unencumbered by checkpoints, makeshift road-blocks, and Jewish-only colonies. From this smooth expanse, we can clearly see the steadily shrinking space available to Palestinians and the suddenly available horizons for exclusivist Jewish Israeli benefit. Internal criticism among Palestinians is necessary but its benefit is contingent on its purpose. There is so much to be critiqued within Palestinian society and especially vis-à-vis their national liberation struggle so that produc-ing a compelling critique seems too easy. The challenge is to articulate a critical perspective with constructive aims rather than paralyzing ones.

Day four (Erez, Sdoud/Ashdod, Jerusalem)

We drove southwest today and reached the western edge of Gaza. We did not have permits to enter so we marveled at the enormous, milita-rized, high-tech crossing known as Erez, one of the five entry points into Gaza, and one of the four controlled by Israel. There, 1.7 million Palestinians are stuck inside a 360-square-mile strip, which the World Health Organization says will be "unlivable" in by 2020. Somehow, though, when US-based mainstream interlocutors speak of security, it is not about the security of the Palestinian residents.

We met Moroccan Jews, or Mizrahim, in present-day Ashdod. It supplants the Palestinian city of Sdoud, whose original residents became refugees upon Israel's establishment and are now stuck in the Gaza Strip. The city is socioeconomically depressed. The speakers discussed their involvement in the Israeli Black Panther party and their oppression and marginalization at the hands of Zionism. They likened themselves to Palestinians, explaining that in 1948, Israel forcibly removed 800,000 *Black* Palestinian Arabs and replaced them with 800,000 *Black* Jewish Arabs. They freely used the term Black to designate themselves and Arabs—a political connection that they draw. They do, however, recognize that Israeli state violence directed at them is quite distinct from that used against Palestinians. Israel continues to ethnically cleanse Palestinians from their land. In contrast, it desires the Mizrahim to stand in as expendable people at Israel's ever-expanding borders and to serve as cheap labor in its market.

Throughout the day American born-and-bred Jewish men, who are now Israeli citizens, discussed their involvement in the human rights movement including with B'Tselem and Rabbis for Human Rights. They emphasized the detrimental features of military occupation like the bypass roads, checkpoints, restricted movements, and most of all, the settlers themselves. Listening to them, one imagines that the entirety of the conflict is neatly contained in the Occupied Territories, as if there were a separate settler economy or a separate Israeli polity specific to the West Bank. Or that only settlers believed that they were entitled to exceptional and privileged treatment because of their Jewish identities, when in fact that conviction is pervasive among all Jewish Israelis, settlers or otherwise. Indeed, what they did not say was more significant than what they did.

They did not discuss how their immigration to Israel is part of the problem, a violent affront on Palestinian lives. Every Jewish immigrant emboldens the state's demographic battle and the justification for its institutionally bestowed, racialized privileges. Nor did they acknowledge the ludicrous notion that the semblance of human rights in the Occupied West Bank and Gaza does not amount to Palestinian self-determination and freedom. Perhaps that makes sense since they are trying to save Israel from itself rather than trying to save themselves from an exclusivist national project.

Day five (Jerusalem, Ramallah)

Today we went to Yad Vashem. It translates into a name and a memorial. In Israel and in the United States it is the Holocaust museum, a site of remembrance of the pain of a state-led genocidal project of Jews in Europe. The horror of the Holocaust, as is well known, has taken on a role far greater than one of memory. It has a political role that is often discounted. A recognition of the Holocaust happens to both disregard the Palestinian Nakba (Catastrophe) and to justify Israeli actions in the present. In Jerusalem, this site of remembrance is built on the remains of a demolished village, Ayn Karem. Just across from it lies the remains of the village of Deir Yassin, where a notorious 1948 massacre took place in which Zionist forces killed 107 Palestinians, including women and children. The massacre was a deliberate attempt to send a message to other Palestinians: that this cold fate awaited them if they did not leave. Today, Deir Yassin is the site of an Israeli mental hospital.

Despite these intersecting layers of violence and pain, the most difficult place to be today was in the car of an Italian journalist as we drove from Ramallah to Jerusalem. I unintentionally cursed at the soldiers at the checkpoint, the arbitrary crossing where Palestinians and others must demonstrate their privilege to enter Jerusalem. I was sincerely sorry for not keeping my cool in the car, as I compliantly flashed my passport and bit my tongue.

The driver, a European journalist, was not happy. She took issue with me jeopardizing her job in Israel and told me to shut up since she had been trying to stay in Jerusalem for the past eight years. Her indignation is rightfully placed. The system is not any less forgiving of her because of her foreign identity. There are rules to obey when traveling in the region; a slight misstep could risk your movement privileges, your career, and your presence. Regardless of your courage, your willingness to sacrifice, your bravado, everyone knows better than to run their mouth at a teenaged soldier at a checkpoint.

Still, I could not wrap my head around her lack of appreciation for the difference between losing one's job and losing one's right to presence. I lost my temper in response to the sympathetic foreign journalist who had no conception of her privilege. My apology was insufficient because it was wrapped up in contempt for the system that now pitted us against one another.

Day six (Lifta, Nazareth)

It is striking how little Israelis know about Palestinians. Not just what they endure but who they are at all. There are few signs that signify the historic presence, agricultural production, commercial trade, or cultural influence of Palestinians. The signs that do exist are under threat of removal because of their threat to a national mythology that this was indeed a land without a people.

Lifta, for example, was home to 2,500 wealthy Palestinians who had two schools and a city center comprised of three spring wells. All of its residents fled by December 1947. We walked through its standing remains, which Israel has declared a nature reserve. Enduring limestone homes sprinkle the landscape. In one home, elaborate marble tiles still line an edge of the floor. High dome-shaped ceilings still provide a cool reprieve from the searing sun. Stairs, doorways, hallways, window frames seem to ricochet with the sounds of playful children's feet. Today, however, that did not concern the Jewish Israeli visitors who swam in one of the spring wells. Nor did it concern the Jewish Israelis who liked to use the abandoned homes to get high or the musicians whose jam sessions benefited from the high-ceilinged hollowed homes. But why should it? Nothing indicated that Lifta was ever home to Palestinians. In fact, most visitors think these homes are Roman ruins.

We continued our journey north to Nazareth, home to the *luckiest* Palestinian citizens of Israel. The city of 80,000 has a vibrant middle class, private schools immune from the Israeli curriculum in which Palestinians do not exist, a recently activated tourist economy, and three hospitals. The *luckiest* Palestinians, however, are also a threat to Jewish dominance and control. So since 1956, Israel has built a settlement to contain, fragment, isolate, and survey the indigenous and numerically inferior citizenry: Netzeret Illit, or Upper Nazareth. The project to over-power the Palestinian population, totaling 50,000 Jewish Israelis, has failed; in response, Upper Nazareth's mayor has consulted Hebron's Settlement Council for advice on how to curb the presence of Palestinians. In a few years' time Upper Nazareth will be home to ideo-logically driven Jews who believe that Palestinians are stealing the land, the land they have always lived on of course. Imagine that Nazareth will soon be home to Hebron-like settlers.

Even the most liberal Jewish Israelis are part of a system that aims to erase, diminish, and marginalize Palestinians and competing narratives in general. The schools are segregated and horribly unequal; the public sector excludes Palestinian employment. The Electric Utility Company employs 30,000 people; six are Palestinian. The Water Utilities Company employs 10,000 people; four are Palestinian.

In Nazareth, we met Sally, a Palestinian woman who facilitates dialogue groups between Israeli and Palestinian women and children within historic Palestine. She explained that in many cases, Jewish children who have Palestinian friends at an early age sever all contact by middle school because their parents fear that their friendships would dilute their enthusiasm for their mandatory Army service. Sally tells us that she had been opposed to dialogue groups for nearly her entire life. A few years ago she changed her mind because she felt that there were few other opportunities to challenge the state's narrative from within.

She recounted how some of the Jewish Israeli children insist that Israel's founding fathers invited Palestinians to stay and live with them but Palestinians chose to leave. It is no surprise that Jewish Israelis think that the whole world is biased against them and picking on Israel. In the obstinate and unchallenged bubble that they live in, that is exactly what it looks like.

Day seven (Jordan Valley, Bethlehem, Dheisheh refugee camp, Nahalin)

The Israeli state apparatus herds Palestinians into enclosed enclaves from within Israel to the West Bank. This violence is not just a restriction on Palestinian freedom of movement; it is tantamount to their captivity. We drove from Nazareth to the Sea of Galilee, headed eastward toward the Jordan Valley, and then southwest to Bethlehem. Along the way we observed the same phenomenon: Israelis forcing Palestinians into concentrated areas, prohibiting them from expanding horizontally, and surrounding them with Jewish settlers and cities. To prevent them from moving beyond their designated ghettos, Israel uses a matrix of laws, civil, criminal, and military, to criminalize their movement.

Nahalin is just fifty kilometers outside of Bethlehem. It is in Area C, which constitutes 62 percent of the West Bank and which remains under full Israeli military and civil control. Nahalin is surrounded by four Jewish-only settlements: Gush Etzion, El'azar, Beitar Illit, and Neve Daniel. Its location, or more aptly, the endurance of its Palestinian inhabitants, disrupts Israel's ethnic cleansing. Because the Nassar family maintained their 1916 land deed, Israel has been unsuccessful in demolishing their homes and removing the family to Areas A or B. Instead, it has cut off their water supply and electricity. Worse, it enables the surrounding Jewish Israeli settler population to violently harass them. In the early 2000s, settlers used bulldozers to place boulders on the main roadway from Nahalin into Bethlehem; it is a makeshift roadblock. Palestinians could easily remove the blocks but doing so comes with an exorbitant fine as well as a criminal conviction and a prison sentence. Instead, the residents trek twenty minutes up and down the hill each way. That is on a good day.

On one, not uncommon, bad day, the settlers uprooted 350 of the Nassar family's olive trees while Israeli soldiers looked on. Today Amal Nassar explained to us that she once ran into a settler woman on her walk home and the woman asked Amal in which settlement she lived. Amal responded that she is Palestinian and she lives in the middle of the settlement ring. The settler woman, with a straight face, said, "No, you don't. No one lives there." Amal must have imagined her existence, or perhaps she read it in a Palestinian textbook.

In Dheisheh refugee camp, a group of young men explained that although the sea is only fifty kilometers away, the only large body of water they ever saw was during a workshop in Germany. They could not travel beyond Bethlehem, which is enclosed on all sides by the Wall. They cannot visit their original villages even for a day. They cannot visit a settlement even if they wanted to. They cannot travel to other Palestinian cities in the West Bank unless they have twelve hours to spare. They certainly could not go to Gaza. Remaining in Palestine for them means remaining in Bethlehem for the rest of their lives. Ibrahim, a psychology and English literature graduate from Bethlehem University, explained, "All I want is choice. The ability to decide where I want to live and how. I am not sure that I would return to my original village if I were given the right of return. I may choose to live in Haifa or Safad instead. But I want to choose. I think choice defines what it means to be human."

In this struggle, the battle is over whether humanity is a zero-sum equation, as ardent Zionists would have us believe, or whether it is infinite as the Palestinian refugees, stuck in one-square-kilometer camps and surrounded by state-sponsored settlers, claim instead.

Day eight (Bethlehem, Bil'in)

Remember the Jordan Valley? It constitutes 30 percent of the West Bank and is fully under Area C; 62 percent of the West Bank is under Israeli civil and military control according to Oslo.

As you travel along the expanse of the Valley, a gravel-paved street divides the stretch of land into two. On one side, acre upon acre of land, as far as the eye can see, is a green ocean of palm trees. Their lush branches dangle with dates that make up a one-billion-dollar settler-colonial industry. On the other side are rolling dunes, parched earth, cacti, and, here and there, a lone resilient palm tree where 400,000 Palestinians used to thrive.

Since 1967, Israel has controlled access to the most significant water sources lying under the West Bank: the northern, eastern, and western aquifers. Sixty percent of the Western Aquifer lies under the West Bank and Israel allocates 80 percent of it for Jewish Israeli use and leaves the rest for Muslim and Christian Palestinians.

The ethnic-based distribution of water is intended to force Palestinians to leave Area C and move to Areas A and B where they can consume (a bit) more water. The Oslo Accords cemented this structural discrimination by disavowing international law and by agreeing to Article 40, which declared all water in the West Bank as Israeli State Property until the elusive Final Status Negotiations. Oslo also created the Joint Water Committee that controls the development of all Palestinian water projects wherein Israel has the right to veto any project. It is no coincidence that today the Palestinian population in the Jordan Valley is 56,000 and dwindling.

In the afternoon, we drove up an unpaved road. When the bus stopped we had arrived in Bil'in. More specifically, we arrived at a slight incline of dirt. At its top, a growing olive tree marked the location where Bassem Abu Rahme took his last breaths after a soldier shot a tear gas canister at his chest from approximate twenty meters away and sent him tumbling down the hill. Bassem was one of Bil'in's many residents whom Israeli forces have killed over the course of eight and a half years of weekly nonviolent actions to protest the confiscation of 2,300 dunums of their land. The state planned on expanding the Modi'in Illit, an illegal settlement for Jewish people only, which, if completed as planned, will be the fourth largest city after Tel Aviv, Jerusalem, and Haifa.

Israel began to build the Wall before it built the rest of the settlement and confiscated Bil'in's lands to do so. Its 1,500 Palestinian residents refused to succumb to the state's dictates or to wait for a broken court system to deliver them justice. After eight and a half years, several fallen martyrs, and countless injuries, the residents compelled the state to change the route of the Wall and won back 1,000 dunams of their land in a struggle memorialized by Emad Burnat's Oscar-nominated film, *Five Broken Cameras*. As we sat under a tree in Bil'in's fields, some movement leaders explained their struggle as being not about the Wall or their lands in Bil'in, but about their freedom throughout all of Palestine.

Day nine (Tel Aviv, Jaffa)

True, Israel may not be the most racist country in the world. It faces stiff competition. But it is incontrovertibly the most self-avowed and self-righteous racist state.

Within Israeli society there is a stark hierarchical order. That order privileges Ashkenazi, or European Jews, above all others, namely Mizrahim (Middle Eastern) and Sephardim (Spanish), non-Jewish Russians, Ethiopian Jews, and well below the last rung on this racial ladder—the Palestinians. The non-white Jewish population is a majority in Israel, but white Ashkenazi Jews control government, capital, and the highest military posts. As put by one of the founders of *Windows*, a Hebrew-Arab youth magazine, "To be accepted in Israeli society, you must be racist . . . the government convinces us that the only way that we can survive is by controlling others."

We saw yet another dimension of this racism in Levinsky Park this morning. Located in south Tel Aviv, the park has become an open-air non-shelter for African refugees who have been granted entry, but not absorbed into Israel. In an effort to whitewash its colonial racism, Israel has admitted entry to nearly 40,000 Sudanese and Ethiopian refugees. It will not, however, consider them for asylum. Instead, Israel pours the non-Jewish asylum seekers into south Tel Aviv, which was already a slum, and is waiting for the right opportunity to return the refugees from whence they came.

Israel is a party to the UN Refugee Convention, and assuming that it has given these persons temporary protection, it should provide them with shelter, education, health care, food aid, and the opportunity to work even if they are not eligible for asylum. Instead, this destitute African population can be penalized for working, though their employers are not punished for employing them. The neighborhood we walked through lacked a single urinal. As we left, one of the delegates lamented that we did not see Tel Aviv; I explained, this *is* Tel Aviv, just not the one Israel wants you to see, like much of the distorted face that it masks.

We were only a few miles away from Jaffa, one of the oldest cities of the world on par with Jericho, and, historically, a beautiful Palestinian port. In early 1948, Jaffa was home to 80,000 to 120,000 Palestinians. As a result of war and an ethnic cleansing project, only 3,000 to 4,000 Palestinians remained after Israel's establishment. We met a descendant of one of those few thousand Palestinians: a twenty-five-year-old leader of the Jaffa Youth Movement. The movement aims to empower Palestinian youth and to resist Israel's efforts to treat them as criminals. He explained that Israelis have criminalized Palestinians for merely existing; "youth wear Reeboks so that they can easily run from the police when they need to."

Elsewhere in Jaffa, the municipal government is supplanting Palestinian landmarks with yuppie consumerist delights. The port, which no longer profits its original fisherman and where farmers no longer sell their infamous oranges, is the site of a series of Israeli artisan shops and exhibits. It seems that the state is eager to physically reconstruct history to ensure Palestinian marginalization and erasure. In Jaffa it is an art exhibit; in the Negev, it will be a forest; in most other places the state erects settlements. Licensed tour guides are unlikely to share this information as the Ministry of Tourism has institutionally denied licenses to Palestinians because of the danger their memory poses to the Zionist project and narrative. Today, of the 9,000 licensed tour guides in Israel, only 300 are Jerusalemite Palestinians. There are no tour guides from Gaza or the West Bank.

Day ten (Hebron)

Hebron is the harshest site of structural and physical violence against Palestinians.

Settlers began to colonize Hebron in 1967 in what they regard as their "homecoming." They are ideologically motivated and are more committed to being on the land, which they believe belongs to *them* by divine decree. Their nonsensical conception of divine real estate is upheld by the presence of three Israeli soldiers and a brandished automatic weapon for each settler, together with complete impunity for their systematic attacks on Palestinians. Unlike other settlements that are built on Palestinian hilltops to facilitate the surveillance and control of Palestinians, the settler community in Hebron is built in the middle of the city. It forms a donut hole that geographically, socially, and economically fragments the entire city. There is nothing holy about Hebron today.

David Wilder, head of the Hebron Settlement Council and a US-born Jewish man from Cleveland, explained that whereas Hebron was off-limits to non-Muslims from 1260 to 1967, today it is accessible to anyone and everyone. He does not mention that as a result of 600 settlers living in the middle of Hebron, the city's 200,000 Palestinians have lost 1,000 homes, have had 1,800 of their businesses closed and confiscated, and must pass through a series of twenty checkpoints within their own city.

Issa Amro, a Palestinian from Hebron and a leader of Hebron Youth Against Settlements, knows David very well. Issa read us a letter that David sent to the Army in which he urges the Israeli military forces to administratively detain the youth activist "for his own good." That is a euphemism for indefinite detention without charge or trial. David wrote the letter after Issa led a march of Palestinians and Israelis wearing face-masks of Barack Obama and Martin Luther King Jr. on the day that Obama landed in Tel Aviv in March 2013. As Obama disembarked his plane, military forces beat and arrested Issa for his peaceful appeal for a just solution.

Issa believes he will be placed under administrative detention soon. The Army arrested him for incitement after he gave an interview to *Al Jazeera Arabic* where he described his group's nonviolent activism. He protests the systematic confiscation of Hebron lands, the criminalization of its Palestinian population, and the policies aimed at forcing its residents to leave. The Old City, for example, has been all but closed.

Palestinians must enter through revolving metal gates common to prisons to enter its narrow streets. Atop the destitute businesses that persevere in the Old City, settlers steadily colonize the rooftops. They throw garbage, stones, and even acid onto the Palestinians below to drive them out.

In response to a question about Baruch Goldstein, the Israeli settler who killed twenty-nine Palestinians as they prayed in the Ibrahimi Mosque in 1994, David explained, "You can count on one or two hands the Jews who have used violence that was not in self-defense." Another delegate asked him about the culture of fear within Israeli society. David, who wore a pistol on his hip, responded, "We don't live in a culture of fear. Everywhere we go we're marked because someone wants to kill us . . . there are people who still want to wipe us out and we cannot depend on anyone else to protect us." He proposes that parents of Palestinian children who throw stones be deported to Lebanon.

Issa, like all other Palestinians, does not have a state, an international force, a pistol, or anyone to protect him. Settlers physically assault, spit on, and expose themselves to Palestinians in Hebron as Israeli soldiers watch. The Army only intervenes if a Palestinian reacts in any way; then, the soldier detains the Palestinian. Issa explains, "I am a nonviolent activist but I believe in defending myself. The problem is that I cannot." Under military law, Issa explains, he is guilty until he can prove otherwise while the Israeli settlers are innocent until proven guilty.

In the Orwellian and apartheid reality of Hebron, self-defense is an ethnically based category.

Day eleven (Jerusalem, Hebron)

It is our final day and we are ending our journey with a closer look at Palestinian women. In conflict, women and children bear the harshest brunt of violence and deprivation. Their existing vulnerability is heightened both within the home as well as beyond its faintly reassuring walls. As Dima Nashashibi of the Women's Centre for Legal Aid and Counseling explained, home demolitions, evictions, and forced displacement are women's issues. Women are especially taxed as they innovatively find ways to provide for their families, to find alternatives to contaminated water, to ensure that their children continue their schooling, and to explain to them the concept of militarized rainfalls. As conflict destroys local and national economies, women are the first to lose employment opportunities. As conflict destroys traditional livelihoods, they must continue to be the trusted conduits of cultural practices and custom. As conflict criminalizes their spouses and children, women remain the steadfast backbone of fragmented families.

Settlement expansion in the South Hebron Hills has exposed its families to extreme state and (state-sanctioned) settler violence. As we drove to At-Tuwani, Hafez explained how the Army declared his community's lands a "Firing Zone," literally a military zone where soldiers practice shooting. Firing zones forcibly displace the Palestinian families who live in them. Israel has designated 18 percent of the West Bank for such practice. Along the way, we passed by the scarred remains of sixty olive trees that settlers had uprooted only weeks before. They left a sign in Hebrew taking credit for their violent attack; they will not be punished. Finally, we arrived at a stone home that belonged to Kifah al-Adarah and her family.

Kifah is a pious Muslim. She sees her role as being a mother, a caretaker of her home, and an aid for her husband and the other men who till their fields. When the Army confiscated a significant swath of their land, and hence the livelihood it provided, her family's income was severely reduced. To make up for that loss, Kifah mobilized At-Tuwani's women to build a handicraft cooperative: They would cross-stitch bags, dresses, pillows, belts, cup holders, tablecloths, and purses and sell them for a profit. The cooperative began with seven women; today it employs thirty-six.

With the money they raised, the women decided to build a school for girls so that they could continue their education beyond the sixth grade. In the course of construction, the Army arrested the men who were building the school. In response, the community decided to continue their activities at night; the men built while the women kept a look out for military patrols. Together, they built one classroom at a time and invited teachers from nearby Tuba to work there. Today the school provides instruction through the eleventh grade.

After finishing her moving story of resilience and incremental triumph, a sympathetic delegate asked Kifah if she would like to reform Islam to improve the status of women. She quickly replied in the negative and explained that Islam afforded her the right to an education as well as to contractual rights within marriage. She fervently defends Islam but derides cultural norms amongst her community.

It is not clear how Kifah reconciles the relationship between religion and culture and, frankly, that is not what we visited her to discuss. Still, the fact that the delegates felt compelled to ask her about her relationship to religion reflects a broader obsession with Palestinian and "Middle Eastern" women more generally. That obsession is fixated on religious reform and women's clothing. This fixation is overly concerned with a warped Eurocentric understanding of women's liberation. Moreover, it works to erase basic political and economic injustices that are constitutive of the societies in which women live.

For example, it makes little sense to discuss women's rights in Gaza without addressing the economic agency necessary to empower a woman to make her own decisions and combat the patriarchy that afflicts her society, not unlike societies the world over. Unemployment in Gaza, which has entered into the sixth year of a comprehensive siege, has reached 32.2 percent and among women it is 77 percent. Addressing women's rights in Gaza should therefore be just as concerned with lifting the siege to improve its economy as it is concerned with her choice of clothing. Bifurcating women's and national rights is a shortsighted exercise. It does not adequately capture the interconnected nature of the oppression faced by Palestinian women and women in general.

Kifah is not troubled by her headscarf. She chose to wear it. She would also like to make a lot of other choices concerning her life and the life of her children but may never be able to as the occupation, settler colonialism, and apartheid tightens their heavy-handed grip.

Extract from *A Concordance of Leaves* (2013)

Philip Metres

قدرو

)

If to Bethlehem we must pass through Wadi Nar

)

If your license plates are painted blue & black

)

If your permit permits no passage across bypass highways

)

If from a distance the road carves alephs or alifs

)

If no man's land is where men live who have no land

)

If you lower your sunshield & block the hilltop settlement

)

If Wadi Nar is the Valley of Fire

)

If we must travel beneath the level of our eventual grave

)

If we arrive & they ask *how are you*, we are to say *thank God*

قدو

)

& though the border guards will advise us
this is a dangerous time to visit

)

& though we had to lie & say we were tourists
& not guests at our sister's wedding

)

to spare ourselves the special interrogation
on the borders of fear / in Ben Gurion

)

& emerge blinking into the light of a modern Oz
beyond the wall / blooming with English lawns

)

the dancers in their purple spangled parachute
pants will turn wheels in the dust until the dust

قدرو

)

is a violet fire & though the checkpoints hunker
in bunkers & Uzis with Uzis will raise them

)

at our unwitting arrival & cause us to lower
cameras & eyes & though hawkers hawk songbirds

)

at Qalandia Checkpoint where garbage bags tumble
free as emptied skulls in No-Man's-Land

)

& the lines of the people are mute with waiting
the *ataaba* singers will arrive in the village

)

& name-check our families *marhaba Metres
marhaba / marhaba Abbadi marhaba*

قدرو

)

& though some seaside café will split into
thousands of shards of glassy dreams

)

& these people will have had nothing to do
with it, & the bulldozers will doze their roads

)

so that every road ends in a wall
every car will pick a path through olive groves

)

& though we won't see the sea the wind
will haul it & the whole village will arrive

)

at the village, until the village will be
a living map of itself, actual size

قرو

)

& though there is a boy whose cheek
is a scar & no father, his eyes like broken eggs

)

the children will flock to every flat roof
to watch the village become the village

)

& see the wedding from enough distance
it looks like a story that could be entered

)

& see the men pin paper money to the suit
of the groom, until he's feathered with future

)

& though everyone will eat, & eat again,
some miracle of loaves & lambs

قدر

)

& though the bride's arms and legs will itch
with arabesques & scripts of henna

)

a second skin won't be scratched away
& though her mother will be angry

)

the women & children will wait
until all the men have been served

)

& even the bride plays a role she only
learns on hennaed heels

)

& though tradition is an invisible
author only the old hands hear

قدو

)

& though the sun will be too bright for the bride
to see much farther than her own eyes

)

& though the bullet in the groom will begin
to hatch in his side, & the stitches in his skull

)

will singe another verse in the book of dreams,
& though the bride's questions will beak their shell

)

years from now, now, now let there be dancing
in circles, let the village become flung arms

)

bringing bodies to bodies & let heads nod
& eyes widen, which we translate as meaning:

قرو

Accept this . . .	تفضل
	tfaddul
Congratulations	مبروك
	mabrouk
How much?	بدك قديش
	addaish badak?
I don't understand	أنا مش فاهم
	ana mish fahim
Tomorrow	بكرا
	bukra
Apricots	مشمش
	mishmish

Tomorrow, when the apricots ripen	في (المشمش) بكرا
	bukra fil mishmish
Tomorrow never comes	في (المشمش) بكرا
	bukra fil mishmish
Ready	ياللا؟
	yallah?
Let's go	ياللا
	yallah

قدرو

)

you my sister you my brother
outside the walls / in the wind

)

if Aristophanes was right
& we walk the world

)

in search of, a split-
infinitive of *to love*, if two

)

outside the walls / in the wind
should find in each other more

)

than mirror, then we should sing
outside the walls / in the wind

)

you my sister you my brother
that tree & stone may answer

)

outside the walls / in the wind
& let *our eccho ring*:

Coda

like strapping a small bomb
to your third finger / that ring

)

about which we could not
speak upon our arrival

)

& departure from the country
of memory where we left you

)

sister / among the fragile
projectiles inside the book

)

whose pages the wind rifles
searching for a certain passage

(Toura, Palestine)

Imagining Myself in Palestine

Randa Jarrar

Trouble began weeks before I boarded my flight to Tel Aviv's Ben Gurion Airport. I had heard horror stories about a detention area there, dubbed the Arab Room, and in my anxious and neurotic style, I had emailed a dozen people—American academics and artists of Arab, Indian, Jewish, and European descent—and asked them what I was supposed to tell the immigration officers at Ben Gurion once I arrived. They all wanted to know if I was using my American passport, and I assured them that I was. The vast majority told me not to tell the officers I would be staying at my sister's in Ramallah. They said this would cause trouble, and offered up the names of friends and family for my use. The generosity of people poured in, and I was advised to say that I was staying with this writer, or that visual artist, or this former IDF soldier—people I had never met, but who had volunteered themselves to be my proxy hosts. A friend of mine, who is a phenomenal photojournalist, gave me her phone number and said to tell the officers I would be staying with her, and I agreed. She told me to prepare for the officers to call her themselves once I gave them her number, as this is something they are known to do.

I was so afraid of facing the guards at the airport that I had a difficult time imagining the rest of my trip. I would picture myself walking around Ramallah with my sister, or attending a concert, or visiting my aunts, or seeing the Separation Wall, or staying at the American Colony Hotel for an evening, and I would draw a blank. There was a wall there, too, between my thoughts and Palestine.

Growing up, my Palestinian identity was mostly tied to my father. He was the Palestinian in the family, and when we went back to the West Bank it was to see his brothers and sisters and parents. We always entered Palestine through Amman, crossing the Allenby Bridge over the river Jordan and waiting in endless inspection lines. I remember these trips dragging on through morning and midday and well into the afternoon. My father would sit quietly, and when I complained my Egyptian mother would tell me that the Israelis made it difficult for us to cross into the West Bank. She told me that they wanted us to give up, that they would prefer we never go back. "We must not let them win," she'd said. My relationship with my Palestinian identity was cemented when I enrolled in a PLO-sponsored girls' camp as a tween. We learned nationalistic songs and dances and created visual art that reflected our understanding of the occupation. After my family and I moved to America in 1991, my Palestinian identity shifted again, and I began to see myself as an Arab American. My father's fiery rants on Palestine died out when Yitzhak Rabin was murdered by a Jewish Israeli extremist. I remember my father weeping in our American wood-paneled den. He said that Rabin had been the Palestinians' last chance.

When my sister got a job in Ramallah last year, teaching music to children, I knew I would want to visit her. I had not been to Palestine since 1993. I had planned to go back in the summer of 1996, but I was pregnant and unmarried. My parents did not want to speak to me, let alone take me with them, in such a shameful condition, to the West Bank. I never went back with family after that. I led my own life. I moved about a dozen times over the following fifteen years—an American nomad. I didn't want to visit the West Bank and be at the mercy of family. If I ever visited, I would do so independently. When my sister moved to

Ramallah she found an apartment of her own, and it had an extra room. It was the perfect time to go. My husband booked my flight, and, thrilled, I told my sister I was coming.

I felt uneasy as soon as I arrived at the gate in Philadelphia. There weren't, as far as I could see, any other Arabs boarding US Airways flight 796 to Tel Aviv. On the airplane, I found myself surrounded by Christian missionaries and evangelicals and observant Jewish men. The group across the aisle had their bibles out, the man sitting next to me read from a miniature Torah, and as the flight took off, I found myself reciting a verse from the Quran, almost against my will. I am an atheist, but all the praying was contagious.

I spoke to no one on the plane, and no one spoke to me, until I got up to stand in line for the bathroom. A man with a wandering eye and a yarmulke asked if I knew why a section of the plane had been hidden behind a thick gray cloth. I said that it was probably to give the flight attendants a little privacy during the eleven-hour trip. He nodded, and said, "Good. I was worried that it was for those crazy ultra-Orthodox people. They're like the Jewish Taliban." I nodded, uncomfortable. I wondered if he would have spoken to me like this if he knew I was of Palestinian descent, and an ex-Muslim. He continued, "They're ruining Israel. They spit on an eight-year-old girl because she was dressed inappropriately." I had heard about that, and told him so. A bathroom opened up, and he moved to slip inside, but before he locked the folding door he said, "Unbelievable how crazy they are."

It was not a conversation I had expected.

As we descended into Israel, the blue Mediterranean floated by below us. We saw the shore of Tel Aviv, and the buildings along it. An American teenager sitting in front of me started shouting, "It's so pretty! It's so pretty!" She wouldn't have any trouble clearing customs, I was sure.

When we landed, everyone on the plane clapped, something I thought only Lebanese people did, and I smiled. I turned on my phone and called my sister and let her know I had arrived, and that I would call her on the other side of customs and immigration. I was only an hour away from her. I took a deep breath and did something superstitious, as

I tend to do when I am feeling powerless and anxious. I flipped to a random page in my passport, hoping to find meaning and reassurance in it. On the page I flipped to was a picture of an old steamship, presumably in the shadow of Ellis Island. I found the image inspiring, calming, and I felt ready to face customs.

I had deleted anything on my website critical of Israel, which amounted to about 160 posts. I had deleted the section in my Wikipedia entry that said that I was a Palestinian writer. It had been unsettling, deleting my Palestinian-ness in order to go back to Palestine. I had been told that the Israeli officers might confiscate my phone and read my Facebook posts and Twitter feed, so I temporarily deactivated my Facebook account and locked my tweets. The entire endeavor left me feeling erased.

I had read an article about the hundreds of activists that had flown into Tel Aviv airport on July 8, 2011. They had all been detained over the weekend and then flown back to their countries of origin. Only one of them had made it through. When she was asked how she managed it, she said that she chose the "smiliest" immigration officer and stood in her line. So, when I entered the immigration hall, I did the same. The agent I chose was blonde and young, and her line was moving the fastest. I stood, waited, and tried to relax.

When there was only one person in the line in front of me, the woman went to the back of her booth and a young bearded man took her place. He did not seem "smiley" at all. I considered switching lanes, but I knew I would look suspicious. So I waited.

When it was my turn, I gave the officer my blue American passport. As he scanned it, I noticed that he had unbelievably long lashes. He thumbed through the pages, and I was afraid of what he would make of the Lebanese stamp. He asked me what my purpose was for visiting Israel. I told him it was my spring break, and I had come to visit friends. He asked me where I was staying. I did as I'd been told, and said I was staying in Jerusalem, with the photojournalist. He picked up a black telephone. When he hung up, he told me to go wait in the room in the corner. I asked him if I could have my passport back, and he said no. I asked him when I would be getting my passport back, and he didn't answer. He only repeated that I needed to go to the room in the corner.

I crossed the immigration hall diagonally, and entered the Arab Room. Sitting in the room and waiting were a young Arab man and an older Arab woman in hijab, two black men in African garb, one of whom was holding an iPad, two middle-aged Arab women in hijab, one dark-haired Tunisian American woman in a long skirt, one woman in a Whitney Houston T-shirt, her hair gathered up in a turban, and one dark-skinned Arab woman in a pant suit. It was readily transparent that we had all been racially profiled. A young man joined us, and got on his phone. I heard him saying, "No, they just finished questioning me. I'm half Egyptian. I should be out soon." I got up and told the woman guard at the door that I needed to go to the bathroom, and she nodded. When I came back to the room, I sat down and took out a magazine, reading as calmly as I could. About twenty minutes passed before a redhead, who couldn't have been older than nineteen, summoned me down the hallway. I followed him to an office where a few brown men were answering questions. The redhead asked me to take a seat and swiped my passport through at his station.

He asked me, "What is the name of your father? And what is the name of your father's father?"

My father and I hadn't spoken since he read my first novel, nearly four years ago. He had sent me an angry email, and told me that we would no longer be seeing one another, or speaking.

I gave the redhead the names he'd asked for. He noted something on a piece of paper, and asked me where my father was from. My father was born in 1950, when the West Bank was part of Jordan, so I told the redhead that my father was a Jordanian American.

"So, he is from Jordania?" the redhead said, and I said that technically, yes. "Where was he born?" he said, and, cornered, I told the redhead that my father had been born in Jenin. He noted something else on a piece of paper, gave it to a man who seemed like a superior, and asked me to go to another room in an opposite corner. When I said that I was a writer and an American citizen, born in Chicago, he shrugged, and instructed me, again, to go to the room in the opposite corner.

I went to the room, and I waited.

My father had said in his email that, by writing about sex in my novel so shamelessly, I had disregarded the legacy of my Palestinian family, which, he claimed, had defeated Napoleon.

I always thought he was being dramatic about Napoleon, but eventually I looked it up. In a book titled *Rediscovering Palestine: Merchants and Peasants in Jabal Nablus 1700–1900*, I found the Jarrar family, and I found Napoleon. The Emperor's attempt to conquer Palestine had been stopped short in 1799, and an ancestor of mine named Shaykh Yousef Jarrar, the mayor of Jenin, had written a poem "in which he exhorted his fellow leaders . . . to unite under one banner against the French forces." I'd never heard of this poet-warrior ancestor before, but I had given my son the middle name Yousef, as if by instinct.

A woman, wearing seven rings on her fingers, and a lot of blue eye makeup caked around her eyes, emerged from a small interrogation room and asked me to join her. She told me to close the door behind me. The room was the size of a walk-in closet, and I knew it had been built to intimidate travelers. The woman said she liked my necklace, and we spoke about jewelry for a few minutes. I admired one of her rings in particular, and she smiled and said it was from Egypt. She then swiped my passport, and asked me about my parents' names, again. This time, I told her I was not in communication with my father, and that I was an American citizen, and a writer. She did not seem to care about this information one way or the other, and spoke my grandmother's name. I hadn't heard my grandmother's name in years. She had died in the early '80s. I told the officer this, and she nodded, and gave me the names of many of my ancestors. I wanted to ask her for her grandmother's name, but gave her the name of my friend in Jerusalem, and my Israeli publisher in Or Yehuda, instead.

"Your publisher?" she said, confused, and I said, yes, my book had been translated into Hebrew and published in Israel. I could see her computer screen. She plugged in my publisher's name and my friend's, in Hebrew, and their addresses came up. The program she was using looked clunky and old, but it held information on every citizen in Israel. At this point, things began to feel Kafkaesque.

She said that there was a Palestinian ID attached to my name. I told her I had no such ID. She said that I had entered the West Bank with the ID in 1993, and that they had record of the entry. She said that this would be a problem. When I tried to plead my case, she asked me to put my right finger on a glowing red scanner. Then my left finger. She took my photograph and asked me to go back to the first waiting room. When I asked her what I should expect, she said she wasn't sure.

Half an hour later, a group of teenage guards took me to baggage claim. I asked them if I could speak to someone from the American embassy, or the consulate, and they nodded, smirking. A few minutes later, I asked them what we were doing there, and they said we needed to find my bag. I said that my carry-on bag was my only bag, and they seemed shocked. I travel a lot, I told them, which they seemed to find suspicious. They asked me why, and I said I was a writer. They frowned at me. We waited for more guards. It must have been their shift change. The baggage claim was deserted. In the corner, a few guards were giving each other massages. The guards I was waiting with gave each other high fives and chatted about teenage stuff. I kept asking what we were waiting for, and they ignored me.

Finally, they took me to a room in the corner of the baggage claim area. It was becoming clear to me that at Ben Gurion, unjust things happened in corners. The guards asked me to open my bags. I did as I was told. I noted that the room was filthy. The Israelis were concerned with showing a clean and gleaming exterior—the floors of the airport outside shone—but for suspected threats and people like myself, behind closed doors, tucked away in dirty corners, they hadn't bothered. A very butch young woman asked me to follow her. She led me to yet another room, where the walls were faded and filthy, and the floor was covered in dirty carpet, littered with small bits of paper and hair clips. It reeked of intimidation, and of humiliation.

I don't believe in hokey things such as souls or spirits, but I could sense a deeply disturbing feeling in the room. There, though I was not strip-searched, the young guard poked and searched every millimeter of my clothes and underclothes. I tried to keep myself distracted, so I wouldn't weep. I tried to keep my spirits up. I wondered if she thought I was a "hair-orist." I did not want to allow these teenagers to rob me of my dignity.

When I came out of the room, a boy with pimples, who looked like he was my son's age, was going through my clothes. Above him hung a tourist poster for the Dead Sea. The poster read: The Dead Sea; Where Time Seems To Stand Still. I had been in Ben Gurion for over two hours, and knew the feeling. It was as if I existed outside of time, suspended in a strange molasses of interrogation.

When he was done checking all my clothes, he asked me if I needed any help repacking the bag. I said that I didn't, and that I had a system for packing. "You have a system?" he shouted. I told him this was an American idiom. Still, he watched me closely as I packed.

I was worn down and angry. The teenagers escorted me back to the waiting room, the Arab Room, where there was now a new guard. A few people were gone, and a few new people had arrived, but it was still an Arab Room.

The woman with all the rings walked in with my passport in her hand and said that she was sorry, but that I was not allowed to enter Israel. She said she had spoken to her supervisor, and that he had decided that I was not to enter. When I asked her if I could speak to him personally, she said she would ask, and walked away with my passport. I never saw her again, nor did I see the supervisor.

I called my sister and told her the news. She was devastated. A friend of mine had been waiting in his car outside the airport to drive me to her, and I called him, too. When I told him now that I was being shipped back to the US, he said, furious, that he would call his friends at the US consulate. When I called him back, he said that there was nothing they could do, and that I was banned by law from entering Israel because I was considered Palestinian.

I told a guard that I was a diabetic, and hungry, and an hour later someone wordlessly brought me the sandwich. I began to feel like a prisoner, grateful for a dry bit of bread and cheese. Halfway through the sandwich, I asked the other people in the room if they were hungry. A middle-aged woman in hijab said she was, and I gave her the rest of the sandwich. A large guard appeared over me, hovering, and asked me in Arabic where I was from. I answered reflexively in English, "I am from here. And from California." He asked me, in Arabic, where I was going after the airport. I said, in English, that I was going to Jerusalem. He walked away and accused me of pretending not to know Arabic. He said the word Arabic hatefully. I followed him, and said, in Arabic, "OK, I do speak Arabic. Where do I want to go after this? I want to go to a bar with my friends." He laughed at me, and said I could go to a bar when I got back to America.

After a while, I was the last person in the room. It had high stonewalls that spanned every floor of the airport, and when I tried to look all the way up, I could not see the ceiling. I felt as if I were trapped in a strange, deep well.

An elderly man who was not Jewish but who had attempted to make aliyah was put in the room with me. When they told him he was being deported back to the US, he said he would not leave. The guard said to him, "I could do this the nice way, or I could do this the not nice way." It was ludicrous in more ways than one, to hear a nineteen-year-old speak to an old man that way. He sounded like a thug.

An hour later, the bearded young man who had originally questioned me at the immigration hall became my guard. When I tried to go to the bathroom, he said I was not allowed. This made me nervous. I had been allowed to go before. I told him so.

"Well, it's different now," he said.

"Different how?" I asked. "Am I under detention?"

He would not answer me. I told him that I was an American citizen and that I demanded to know whether or not I was under detention. He closed his eyes, then opened them, and said, reluctantly, "Yes."

I lost it. I demanded to see someone from the embassy or the consulate. He ignored me. I said that he needed to take me to the bathroom.

He said no. I lifted up my dress and pretended to squat, and shouted, "Fine, then I will go to the bathroom right here!"

He became angry and shouted to another guard to take me to the bathroom. When she said she couldn't, he took me himself. He insisted on the gender-neutral handicapped toilet, and he waited outside the stall. When I was done, he checked the stall after me, to make sure that I had not concocted a bomb out of my pubic hair. I laughed at him, and he angrily took me back to the detention room.

I waited two more hours. Whenever a guard came into the room, I would ask him what was going on with my passport, and what I could expect. The guard would look down at me and sneer, "You have to wait. You have to wait." When I told him I had been waiting for hours, he only repeated, "You have to wait." My wait felt interminable. In his speech to the UN, Mahmoud Abbas quoted the late Palestinian poet Mahmoud Darwish's poem, "State of Siege." He read,

> Standing here. Sitting here. Always here.
> Eternally here,
> we have one aim and one aim only: to continue to be.

And he added, "And we shall be." The state of sitting, of standing, of waiting, is the principal state of the Palestinian; it is the state of the refugee, of the oppressed, of the outsider, of the writer.

Eventually, two female guards came to tell me what time I would board the flight back to the US. When they did, I burst into tears. I had been holding out hope, right to the last. After they left, I was stuck with the male guard again, the one who had picked up the phone in the immigration booth.

I asked him if I could board a flight elsewhere—to Amman, or Cairo, even Paris. I wanted to go somewhere, at least, even if I couldn't see my sister. "No," he said. "You have to go back from where you came." I said that this was unacceptable, and that I wanted the choice to go elsewhere. This time, he shouted it. "No. You must go back from where you came."

"Are you from *The Lord of the Rings*?" I said.

He narrowed his eyes at me, and snapped, "Come with me." He made me stand in a hallway for twenty minutes, as punishment. I made fun of his long eyelashes. I asked him if he was related to Snuffleupagus. He ignored me. An hour or so passed, and a guard came and eventually escorted me to flight 797, back to the US. We bypassed security, avoiding a scene, and when we got to the airplane the guard gave my passport to the flight attendant, an American.

"Do not give her back her passport until you arrive in America," he said. She squinted at him, confused. "What do you mean?"

"This woman was denied entry, and must return to the United States. Do not give her this passport until you have left Israel and arrived in America." She looked at me and nodded, frowning.

I went to my seat, which was in the middle of the middle row, the worst place to sit on a twelve-hour flight. The flight attendant walked over and handed me my passport. "Um, here you go," she said, and I laughed and thanked her.

Holding my passport again on that almost-empty plane, I understood, in a way, how lucky I had been. The passport hadn't been confiscated. I was not imprisoned. And yet, this was how Israel treated someone with a voice and American citizenship. There are today, held without charge in the Israeli military detention system, hundreds of Palestinians, including children. There are reports of a systematic pattern of ill treatment toward them. Silenced and oppressed, these prisoners have little recourse. In the news recently I saw that 2,000 of these prisoners have resorted to the last form of protest left to them: They have collectively gone on hunger strike.

I flipped through the passport, and, surprised, found that the officials had left a stamp on it. The stamp was massive, and read, in English and Hebrew, Ben Gurion Airport ENTRY DENIED. I stared at it for a few minutes. Then, I saw it: the picture of the ship I had seen eight hours earlier, that I had thought was a sign of good luck.

I remembered how, when I first met my mother-in-law in Texas, we had bonded over her collection of costume jewelry. A lot of the pieces were from her first husband, whom she had divorced before meeting my father-in-law. I noticed that many of the pieces he'd given her had imagery of boats and ships. When I pointed that out to her, she had raised her wine glass and said, "You're right! He was shippin' me out." And that's what had happened to me. I had been shipped out.

Two massive, bald-headed men sat on either side of me. If I believed the conspiracies, I would have thought those guys were Mossad. But it was obvious before long, from the way they blasted terrible club music on their earphones and, later, passed out, that they were just some doofuses on their way to America. In an attempt to be polite and not touch the men around me, I folded my arms, but this became terribly uncomfortable after a while. A few hours into our flight, I decided that I was tired of being polite and so I put both my arms down. Minutes later, the man on my right began to jab my elbow. I ignored him and feigned sleep. He jabbed and jabbed.

Finally, I turned to him, my arm firmly on the armrest, and said, "I get it."

He looked at me, embarrassed.

"I really get it. But I am keeping this armrest. I am not moving. I will keep my arm here for the rest of the flight," I said. And I did.

Checkpoint

Jasiri X

Journal of the hard times tales from the dark side
Evidence of the settlements on my hard drive
Man I swear my heart died at the end of that car ride
When I saw that checkpoint welcome to apartheid
Soldiers wear military green at the checkpoint
Automatic guns that's machine at the checkpoint
Tavors not M16s at the checkpoint
Fingers on the trigger you'll get leaned at the checkpoint
Little children grown adults or teens at the checkpoint
All ya papers better be clean at the checkpoint
You gotta put ya finger on the screen at the checkpoint
And pray that red light turns green at the checkpoint

If Martin Luther King had a dream of the checkpoint
He wake with loud screams from the scenes at the checkpoint
It's Malcolm X by any means at the checkpoint
Imagine if ya daily routine was the checkpoint

Separation walls that's surrounding the checkpoint
On top is barbwire like a crown on the checkpoint
Better have ya permits if ya found at the checkpoint
Gunmen on the tower aiming down at the checkpoint
The idea is to keep you in fear of the checkpoint
You enter through the cage in the rear of the checkpoint
It feels like prison on a tier at the checkpoint
I'd rather be anywhere but here at this checkpoint
Nelson Mandela wasn't blind to the checkpoint
He stood for free Palestine not a checkpoint
Support BDS don't give a dime to the checkpoint
This is international crime at the checkpoint
Arabs get treated like dogs at the checkpoint
Cause discrimination is the law at the checkpoint
Criminalized without a cause at the checkpoint
I'm just telling you what I saw at the checkpoint
Soldiers got bad attitudes at the checkpoint
Condescending and real rude at the checkpoint
Don't look em in they eyes when they move at the checkpoint
They might strip a man or woman nude at the checkpoint
Soldiers might blow you out of ya shoes at the checkpoint
Gas you up and then light the fuse at the checkpoint
Everyday you stand to be accused at the checkpoint
Each time your life you could lose at the checkpoint

If Martin Luther King had a dream of the checkpoint
He wake with loud screams from the scenes at the checkpoint
It's Malcolm X by any means at the checkpoint
Imagine if ya daily routine was the checkpoint

At the airport in Tel Aviv is a checkpoint
They pulled over our taxi at the checkpoint
Passport, visa, ID at the checkpoint
Soldiers going all through my things at the checkpoint

I was high risk security at the checkpoint
Because of the oppression I see at the checkpoint
Occupation in the third degree at the checkpoint
All a nigga wanna do is leave fuck a checkpoint

Below Zero: In Gaza Before
the Latest War

Ben Ehrenreich

The passport terminal at Erez Crossing is like the airport of your very worst dreams. There are no duty-free shops on the other side, no airplanes, no runways, and no possibility of flight, just a series of cages opening finally into the biggest cage of all, the Gaza Strip. The terminal is a cavernous building constructed entirely of metal and glass. High-ceilinged, with beams and ventilation ducts exposed. Everything is sterile. A row of blue tollbooth-like structures divides the hall in two. Nearly all of them are empty. If you linger too long, a sunglassed fellow carrying a Tavor submachine gun will stroll by to grunt you in the right direction. You will stand before a glass door and wait for a light to turn green. When it does, you will pull the door open and push your documents through the slot to the Israeli official inside the booth.

Only a very few categories of humans are permitted to pass in either direction through Erez: foreign journalists, select international aid workers, a small number of Palestinian officials and businessmen, and those lucky Palestinians approved to seek urgent medical care unavailable in Gaza. It was April 2014 when I crossed: seventeen months since the most recent bombardment, three months before the next one. Fifteen weeks before the shelling of the el-Wafa Rehabilitation Hospital in Gaza City, fifteen and a half weeks before the four boys were blown to pieces while playing on the beach by the seaport, sixteen weeks before the ground invasion and the massacres in Shuja'iyya and Khuza'a and the shelling of the Al-Aqsa Martyrs Hospital in Deir al-Balah, seventeen weeks before the massacres in Rafah and the shelling of the al-Shifa Hospital in Gaza City and the killing of eight children playing in the street in a single missile strike on the al-Shati refugee camp, eighteen weeks before the destruction of the 1,365-year-old al-Omari Mosque in Jabalia, twenty weeks before the death toll crossed 2,000, twenty-one weeks before, after the leveling of the fifteen-story al-Basha tower in Gaza City, the ceasefire finally stuck. None of that had happened yet. I didn't know it then, but these were good days.

The woman behind the glass was polite, warm even. She inspected my press card, my passport and visa. She asked me how long I would be staying in Gaza. She asked my father's name, and his father's name. For a moment, my grandfather, dead for fifteen years, hovered behind my shoulder. He was laughing. I was glad for his company. The woman behind the glass returned my documents. "Have a nice trip," she said, and smiled.

I collected my things and waited for the photographer friend with whom I was traveling. We passed through a tall metal turnstile, and then another, into a concrete-walled room. Several low, steel doors without knob or latch or peephole were set into one wall. All were closed. I looked for an exit. There was none. The turnstile only turned one way. We waited. Surely someone knew that we were here? They did. One of the steel doors slid suddenly open. We walked through it. The door shut behind us with a clank. We were in Gaza now, in an open space with a concrete floor, a metal roof, and walls of wire mesh. The walls narrowed into a tunnel stretching off into the distance. I had heard about this part: the kilometer-long cage. There was nothing to do but walk.

To our right was the wall separating the Gaza Strip from Israel, constructed here as in the West Bank of slabs of concrete about six meters high and a meter and a half wide. For a short stretch beside the terminal, erosion had caused the wall to collapse. A storm the previous winter had washed away the sand and the slabs lay jumbled and broken, pointing in odd directions, like bad teeth. Then the tunnel turned south, toward Gaza City. On both sides of the cage, the fields were bright with wildflowers. To the left a flock of sheep was grazing. Camels wandered freely a little farther off. Birds perched in the wire mesh, chirping as they took flight. A vehicle was approaching, a mutant motorcycle-drawn tuk-tuk hauling giant suitcases. The driver sped by without making eye contact. A golf cart passed behind him with two veiled women in the backseat: the inter-cage taxi service.

At last the tunnel opened onto a courtyard, where we handed our documents to a Palestinian Authority official sitting behind a window cut into a shipping container. He handed them back, and we got into a taxi (full-sized). "Welcome," the driver said after a short drive to the final checkpoint. "It's a beautiful day," he said. And it was. We presented our documents to a Hamas policeman sitting behind yet another window. After a few minutes of confusion—my papers handed off to one man in plain clothes, and then another—he handed me my passport and a Hamas-issued permit allowing me to stay in the Gaza Strip for one week. I had arrived.

The night before, US Secretary of State John Kerry had flown off to Brussels, precipitously canceling a scheduled meeting with Palestinian Prime Minister Mahmoud Abbas. Kerry's seemingly indefatigable optimism had cracked. The negotiations were scheduled to continue for another three and a half weeks, but Israeli commentators were already discussing them in the past tense. For the previous eight months, at Kerry's urging, Israeli and Palestinian negotiators had been talking— mainly they had been talking about talking, and talking about what they would have to talk about if they were ever to begin talking about talking in earnest. Possible land swaps between Israel and the West Bank had come up. So had the fate of Jerusalem, of the major settlement blocs, and of the Jordan Valley. Entirely absent from the conversation, though, was Gaza and the 1.7 million Palestinians who live in the Strip's scant

139 square miles, fenced in by concrete and razor wire, watched from above by Israeli drones and surveillance balloons.

The people of Gaza have been trapped, isolated, forgotten by the world—except when Israel chooses to bomb them with more than the usual fervor—since 2007, after Hamas, which had won the Palestinian legislative elections one year earlier, pushed out Abbas's Fatah party and took control of the Strip. Israel imposed a blockade, severely limiting the transport of goods in and out, strangling Hamas by starving its constituents. The goal, as Dov Weisglass, senior advisor to then Prime Minister Ehud Olmert, said in 2006, was to "put the Palestinians on a diet, but not to make them die of hunger." Two years later, the Israeli authorities drew up secret guidelines, calculating the minimum caloric intake of Gaza residents and determining on that basis the precise quantities of food that they would allow to enter the Strip. In the meantime, except when the bombs were falling, Gaza all but disappeared. It became the dark side of the promised land, just out of sight, rarely mentioned and seldom heard, not part of any proposed solution, a perpetual problem that has been and will continue to be contained. Gaza's present is one possible future—not just for the West Bank, if things continue on their current path, but for the rest of the world, wherever entire populations are unwanted and feared, wherever the resources exist to control them from above.

The streets of Gaza City were dusty and gray. Ragged green flags fluttered on the lampposts. In some neighborhoods more than half of the buildings looked unfinished, their concrete-blocks un-stuccoed and, except for the ubiquitous graffiti, unpainted. Even in the busiest downtown streets, traffic was light: Fuel prices have doubled since the Egyptians shut down the smuggling tunnels in the summer of 2013, depriving Hamas of its tax base and cutting the flow not only of weaponry but also of livestock, home appliances, clothing, construction materials, medicine, gasoline, food. Every third or fourth storefront was shuttered. Banners hung from rooftops commemorating martyrs, advertising the courage and sacrifice of one armed faction or another. They were crude photoshopped pastiches, the face of a smiling young man, now dead, beside another image of the same boy, posing proudly with a rifle. Billboards hawked air conditioners, savings accounts, insurance. Horses and donkeys trotted below them through the streets, pulling carts. Many of the shops appeared to have nothing in stock but a single shelf of motor oil. Others displayed their wares on the sidewalk: crates of oranges; plastic toys; red-and-green-labeled bottles of Coca-Cola and Sprite; car batteries; chickens; used bumpers and doors.

We drove east and out of the city until there were open fields and olive groves on both sides of the road. We passed abandoned gas stations and idle factories. Moharam Fouad worked a small plot of land, turning over the soil with a short-handled hoe. He wore Adidas track pants, the knees dark with dirt. His wife sat cross-legged on the ground a few yards away, a child in her lap. Fouad had owned a house near here, he said, but the Israelis bulldozed it on the second day of Operation Cast Lead in December 2008. (More than 3,000 Gazan families lost their homes in that brief and one-sided war; thirteen Israelis and 1,400 Palestinians, mostly civilians, were killed.) Since then, Fouad and his family have lived in a mud-walled hut. His wife was pregnant. The land he was tilling wasn't his. He was paid twenty shekels a day to farm it, he said, a little less than six dollars. He used to work in the tunnels and made nearly four times as much. The child stood at Fouad's feet, sucking a finger and clinging to his leg. Fouad smiled. "It's like life below zero," he said. Far to the north, a white balloon hung high in the sky, watching.

We got back in the car and drove east toward the Buffer Zone. On the other side, in Israel, the fields were furrowed with crops, but here mainly grass and yellow wildflowers grew. The land that Mohammad al-Dabba was farming was a rare exception. He was an older man, dapper in a brown vest and gray button-down shirt. He smoked a cigarette in a wooden holder, picking at the spines of a paddle cactus with his free hand. In 2009, Israeli planes dropped leaflets warning Gazans not to come within 300 meters of the border fence. The IDF, the fliers promised, would "eliminate anyone who will be found in the zone . . . Since you are warned, no excuses are accepted." The UN estimates that 30 percent of Gaza's arable land has been lost to the Buffer Zone. (During the last war, the Buffer Zone expanded to comprise 40 percent of the entire Gaza Strip.) Israeli troops "shoot on a daily basis," al-Dabba said, as if he were talking about the weather. "It depends how close we get."

One of al-Dabba's sons, he said, had been shot in the eye. Not in the Buffer Zone, but during an incursion by Israeli troops twelve years ago. He was a boy, and had been throwing stones at soldiers. The bullet had passed through the back of his head, but he survived, al-Dabba said, praise God. (I would meet him later, a quiet, muscular man with a long, black beard, wearing jeans belted with a brass buckle that said, "Hell on Wheels." The right side of his face was scarred but handsome, the eye dark and intense. His left eye was shriveled and dead.) Another of al-Dabba's sons had been shot in the leg. And just a few weeks ago a farmer named Ibrahim Mansour was shot dead—al-Dabba pointed to the border—"right over there." A flock of crows took flight two fields over. In the distance, a military Jeep crawled along the line. Al-Dabba pulled a phone from his pocket to see if anyone from Mansour's family was around.

He walked across his field, and we took the road and met him in the yard of an adjacent cement factory. The wall of the warehouse beside it was scarred with gunfire, and with larger holes from some more substantial form of artillery. No one appeared to be working in either facility. Al-Dabba brought out plastic chairs for us to sit on, tea for us to drink. Salaama Mansour arrived on the back of a friend's motorbike. Ibrahim had been his brother-in-law. He was killed on the 13th of February, Salaama said. He had gone out with a few others, collecting gravel to sell to the cement plants. Ibrahim was a farmer, but there's little work in farming anymore—the blockade keeps external markets inaccessible, and the local markets are flooded with cheap Israeli produce—so he gathered stones instead. On a good day, he could make between ten and twenty shekels, about three to six dollars.

That day, the soldiers first fired tear gas to disperse the workers. They got out of their Jeep, Salaama said, and took shelter behind some high point where the workers couldn't see them. The soldiers appeared to have left, so the workers returned. "When they came out they shot him," Salaama said. Another man was shot in the foot. He lived. Ibrahim didn't. "The bullet exploded inside his head." He was thirty-eight. He left seven children. "It was normal that he would be shot," Salaama said.

We returned to the city and drove to the home of Hussam Salama. It was easy to find. A huge banner hung outside the house depicting Salama, a thin-faced man with short hair and a light beard, and Mahmoud al-Kumi, who was beside him in the car when their vehicle was struck by an Israeli missile during the last major bombardment, on November 20, 2012, one day before the ceasefire. Both men were journalists for the Hamas government's Al-Aqsa television network. Salama's father, Mohammed, met us in the courtyard. He sat bent in a plastic chair. He was white-haired, long-limbed, so thin that his clothes looked like they'd been hung on him to dry.

His son was a cameraman, he explained. "There was shelling in this area, and he came to film." When he was done, he stopped at home to eat, but "there was more shelling, and he left to go and see. The car was targeted. He was on his way back to the office. The rocket set the car on fire. The more water we put on it, the higher the flames rose." He didn't know if the missile that killed his son had been fired by a fighter plane or by one of the drones that hover constantly above the Strip. (Estimates vary widely, but at that point, between 600 and 1,100 Palestinians had been killed in drone attacks since 2000, most of them civilians. The number has since risen substantially.) It didn't matter. The result was the same.

I had read about Salama's and al-Kumi's deaths when they occurred, though I had never learned their names. I was in California, anxiously following events in Gaza on Twitter and the internet. The journalists' car was clearly marked — "TV" written on the roof in neon letters so that it could be seen from above. It was traveling behind another press vehicle carrying a driver and fixer employed by the *New York Times*. In an article published that evening, the *Times* devoted one sentence to the incident, nineteen paragraphs down, without suggesting that there was anything anomalous about assassinating journalists.

The old man was weeping silently, twisted in his chair, his legs crossed and his knees pulled almost to his chest. His son was thirty years old, he said, and had four children, two boys and two girls. "Everybody loved him," he said. "Everywhere he went he was loved and adored. Thousands of people came to his funeral." He wiped at his eyes and nose with a tissue. The tears kept coming. I asked if there was anything else he wanted to say.

He nodded. "May God take revenge on them."

The sun was getting low, the light soft. We went to the beach. The sea seemed a deeper blue than it had the day before when I had seen it from the other side of Erez, in Israel. The fishing boats were leaving the pier, setting out for the night's work. I could just barely make out three Israeli gunboats, gray shadows bobbing on the waves a few hundred meters offshore. Kids played soccer on the trash-strewn sand. The older boys practiced parkour, hurling their bodies in the air, flipping and twirling with astonishing ease. They had constructed a springboard by laying a sandbag atop a half-buried tire. One of them kneeled beside it, guiding and encouraging the younger kids, teaching them to jump and flip. They took running starts, one by one, landing on their buttocks and knees with great, giggling splashes of sand. The sun sank lower. Farther down, four young men were throwing fishing nets onto the beach, gathering the weighted nets and tossing them, then doing it again, catching only air and sand. A horse galloped through the surf, a cart towed behind it. The driver stood balanced on the carriage, surfing it, his arms raised to the sky, screaming with joy, splashing through the waves to join his friends.

In the morning we came across another horse. It was lying on its side on the asphalt, a block from the shore, in the al-Shati refugee camp. Two men stood above it, a policeman and the horse's owner, a middle-aged man in a brown canvas cap with a leather bill. The horse had just collapsed. Its chest was heaving, its veins tight. Its flesh was almost purple beneath a thin layer of gray and white hair. I found a bottle of water in the car and handed it to the horse's owner. He poured it over the animal's ears and face, rubbing it into the horse's neck. The horse lapped at the water pooling around its lips.

A few boys gathered round to watch, and two young men. One of them, at the owner's direction, hooked a rein to the horse's bridle and began to pull at its head. The owner slapped the horse lightly, saying, "Yalla, yalla" ("come on, let's go"). He pried one of the horse's feet out from under it and placed it square on the pavement. The young man did the same with the other front foot. They heaved at the rein, trying to drag the animal to its feet, succeeding only in lifting its giant head from the ground. The horse resisted. Its head snapped back and thwacked hard against the asphalt. The sound seemed to echo. The men were still for a moment. Blood from a cut on the horse's knee streamed into the street. The men tried again, lifting the horse's feet, pushing it up, slapping its face with the rein. "Yalla, yalla." But the horse collapsed again and rolled over on its back, its feet lolling limp in the air. There was something indecent about it. The men pushed it onto its side again. Another cut had opened on one of the horse's legs.

By now a small crowd had gathered. Everyone stood in silence, arms crossed or cocked against hips. A boy showed up hauling a bucket. A man brought two soda bottles filled with water. The owner knelt and splashed the water over the horse's withers and belly and flanks and rump, cleaning its wounds with an anxious tenderness, rubbing the cool liquid into the animal's purple flesh. The horse reared, lifting its head, and everyone around it took three steps back. Its eyes were panicked—it had recovered enough to feel fear. But panic took too much energy. It didn't last. More buckets came. The owner wandered across the street to make a phone call. Children watched from a third-story window. Flies gathered on the animal's wounds. The horse raised its head, slowly this time, and looked around as if it were searching for someone it knew. When we left, except for the occasional twitch of its eye and its ears, the horse was lying still. Its owner and the young man who had been helping him were sitting on the curb beside it, staring at the street between their knees.

Gate of Freedom

Deema K. Shehabi

For Palestinian hunger striker, Samer Issawi

Lovers of asparagus, alive
as hummingbirds, place their nostrils
over a low cloud, wet of air.
It's the year of green hills
in California that early spring;
the evening is blue-split between the first
snow on the mountain top,
and a computer screen, where news of a man
whose body is eating itself, scythes
the long-stemmed breaths in the room.
"Do not weep if my heart fails," he writes.
"I am your son."
  Gate of Love
Son I have. Your hands bulge
with pear tree blossoms.
You are bellow and sweat,
hunger and bread.
I part the fog to find you

through a grimy crowd of kids.
Before you give in to the affection
that soils you in public,
I'll promise you a truce.
        Gate of the Sun
Bristling down the chemical-
scraped hall uttering
assalamu alaikums to the young
patients from the UAE, their heads sagging
to the side, their bodies a shrine
to tumors, husks of overgrown cells,
the chemo fountain. One boy
stares through a sieve
of darkness, hewn around dark-gray clouds.
        Gate of Peace
"I have so many sons withering,"
I whisper to the Chinese elm, as news
of the man whose body is eating itself,
disputes with the bresaola on crisp baguette
that I'm eating in a garden

among the flung-out
blue jays and limping Daddy long legs.
No hymns left;
only a small neck
the sun gnarls through.

Soundtracks of the Resistance

Rumzi Araj

My mother was born in Gaza. A United Nations report just said that Gaza might be "uninhabitable" by 2020. It's hard to think of Gaza as a refuge for anyone. But for my mom and her family, that's exactly what Gaza was: a refuge. My grandparents left their home in Beit Jala in 1949 for Gaza City, leaving with an Egyptian Army Caravan out of the West Bank. My grandfather had been arrested for organizing in opposition to Jordanian control of the West Bank after the war with Israel ended in 1949. After my grandmother somehow secured his release in the middle of the night, they left everything behind and took off as soon as they could. My grandmother was pregnant on the journey and eventually gave birth to three of her six children in Gaza, my mother included. Though Beit Jala, a small town just up the hill from Bethlehem and the birthplace of my father, is the place that would become my mother's home, the first three years of her life were spent in Gaza. After she and her family returned to Beit Jala in 1954, no one in our family had ever gone back to Gaza.

Then one day, nearly fifty years later, my cousin Jackie Salloum heard Palestinian hip-hop being played on a New York public radio station and we decided we needed to go back.

I was born in a small town in Ohio, shockingly the only Palestinian family in town. Like most Palestinian Americans, though, my family ensured that I developed a strong Palestinian identity. I was raised on stories like the one of my family's brief exile from Beit Jala and the more permanent ones to the United States, Honduras, Chile, and Ecuador, among other countries. I watched the First Intifada on TV with my parents, getting shushed every time I tried to speak over the news coverage. I learned that my family back home in Palestine had it better than many other Palestinians and I just felt lucky to be sitting in Ohio while many cousins my age were stuck in the West Bank. I read as much as I could about our history and the conflict. I wanted to know as much as possible. Still, despite my family's history there, I knew shamefully little of Gaza. Though I had traveled to Palestine with my family twice as a child, it wasn't until we started filming *Slingshot Hip Hop*, a documentary film on the emerging Palestinian hip-hop scene in Gaza, the West Bank, and inside Israel that I fully understood what being Palestinian meant. That's what happens when you go to Gaza.

Jackie and I were so excited to show the world that Palestinians were doing something cool: hip-hop. After years of trying to explain the Palestinian-Israeli conflict using facts and figures about refugees, destroyed villages, checkpoints, settlements and so on, I heard in the passion and intensity of these lyrics set to a beat everything I had been trying to convey. As one older radio call-in listener from Gaza said after he heard Palestinian hip-hop for the first time, "With all the partying and dancing they will memorize the hell out of it. Soon all Americans will be singing our words!" A little overly optimistic, yes; but, still, it was exciting. And it wasn't just any hip-hop, it was hip-hop that would make the South Bronx proud. Over mostly bootlegged beats, the lyrics were about struggle, resistance, and survival. It was filled with anger and hope. We rushed over to Palestine as soon as we could to start filming.

I traveled to Palestine several times for the production of *Slingshot Hip Hop*, from 2003 to 2007, but it wasn't until my second trip in 2005 that I finally made it into Gaza. Getting into Gaza was hard, but almost laughably easy compared to the situation today, where humanitarian aid can barely get in. But still, the Palestinian hip-hop artists inside Israel that became the subjects of the film had never met any of the guys doing the same thing in Gaza. You had to get special permission from Israel to get in, and it was almost never given. Most often though it's people trying to get out of Gaza, not get in. And for Palestinians in Gaza, you could wait a lifetime to get permission to leave that probably won't ever come. Because the artists in Gaza were so isolated from their contemporaries in the West Bank and Israel, it was even more important that we get there, both to include their story as a crucial component of the film and to help facilitate a connection with other Palestinian rappers outside Gaza. Although it was incredibly difficult for us to gain access to Gaza, we had a far better chance of getting in than the Palestinian MCs we had met in the West Bank and Israel. In fact, Gaza was so isolated that the Palestinian MCs in Israel didn't even know that Palestinian hip-hop existed in Gaza until they saw the footage. They were floored, especially by how much the Gazan MCs idolized them and tried to emulate them.

The crowd that packed the Red Crescent Society for the first hip-hop show in Gaza looked like a family reunion. There were young and old, men and women, and of course lots of kids. The initial shock of what was happening onstage soon turned into rousing cheers and everyone clapping to the beat. There was even break dancing. At one point the crowd, filled with pride, started chanting, "GA-ZAAAA . . . GA-ZA! GA-ZAAA . . . GA-ZA!" For a few minutes in that building, Gaza didn't look very different from the rest of the world. But Gaza is different. And I wanted to see it for myself.

After months of planning and weeks of uncertainty, Jackie and I received permission to enter through a contact with a local NGO. On our way to the Erez checkpoint, the single entrance from Israel to Gaza, we still had no idea if we would be able to get in. We had heard endless stories of people getting turned away from Gaza and, after our own seven-hour detention and interrogation at Ben Gurion Airport, we expected the worst. After a couple of hours' delay and relatively minor questioning from the Israeli soldiers, we were sent on our way, carrying our equipment on our backs through an almost mile-long checkpoint crossing. When we got to the other side, it was like the curtain had been pulled back from a lifetime of watching Gaza on the world stage.

We immediately took a taxi to a barbershop in Gaza City where one of the young hip-hop artists from the group Palestinian Rapperz (PR) worked. He demanded that he give me haircut, even though I didn't want one. I obliged, or I should say, lost the argument. Sitting in that barber chair with pictures of '90s boy bands and Versace models hanging all over the walls, I kept on thinking, "How bad can Gaza be?" Looking back now, after multiple Israeli attacks that destroyed entire city blocks, killed thousands of civilians, and blockaded the entire Gazan population from the rest of the world, the answer is: really, really bad. But while I was sitting in that chair, the only thing I knew for certain was that I wasn't going to let this young hip-hop barber glob on the enormous amount of hair gel he was holding over my head.

Hair gel became a major theme of the trip in Gaza. One of the main artists in the film, Mohammad from PR, was on a constant search for the best hair gel. He must have bought three jars in the weeks we were there. Mohammad had been shot in the arm by Israeli soldiers at a protest a few years before, but it was as if the one thing he cared about, the one thing he could be in charge of within the confines of total Israeli control of his life, was the stability of his hairdo. And gel was his weapon. He was going to win.

Everything in Gaza becomes relative. Just when I would start to feel bad for someone, we would be introduced to someone who had it much worse. It was sort of a microcosm of Gaza as a whole. Just when you think things can't get worse there, it does. On levels that make the old bad seem good and the old good seem totally out of reach. When we met Ibrahim though, I was sure that I had seen the worst.

Ibrahim was a late-teenage MC who collaborated with PR and others in Khan Yunis and Gaza City. He dressed "baggy," as all the guys liked to call their style of dress, with ridiculously oversized clothing that made American hip-hop artists seem like they were wearing slim-fitting clothing. He was tall and athletic and liked to play basketball. Ibrahim seemed like a pretty normal kid. When he took us to see where he lived I wasn't prepared for what I would see. He lived in the Nemsawy refugee camp on the outskirts of Khan Yunis. This was like the curtain behind the curtain. It looked post-apocalyptic. There weren't streets; just sand and the rubble of buildings that had had missiles dropped right through the center of them. The buildings that were still standing looked like someone had used their facades as target practice. I tried not to react and pretended that I wasn't shocked that people still lived in these buildings. I had been to Palestinian refugee camps before, in the West Bank and in Lebanon, but this looked like another world. It's hard to use words to describe Gaza. I want people to see it, to feel it, to smell it. To know the depths of the devastation but also the depths of the steadfastness of the people too. Luckily, that's what Ibrahim was able to do with his music.

It's hard not to feel like a voyeur in those situations, when you are passing through someone's difficult circumstances and asking to film it. Isn't that what Gaza has become? Just another thing that we watch happen, over and over again, the horrors of each new Israeli assault just another passing headline that we care about as long as the news tells us it's important. In between the bombings, daily life continues, and these daily realities matter. Among the day-to-day lives in Gaza are the stories of young people using a creative form of resistance in the face of seemingly insurmountable oppression. Every time I think of Gaza, I think of the people I met there and how much worse it has gotten since my visit in 2005. I think back to every home I was invited into for tea or coffee by friends of friends or even strangers and how happy they were to share what little they had, their pride unwavering even under sometimes impossible circumstances. I think of Ayman, one of the MCs from PR, whose father was recently killed by an Israeli missile while sitting in his living room, and the firefighters who were killed by a second missile as they tried to rescue people from the building. It is a reminder of how close every person we met, and every person in Gaza is, to death. In one of the most densely populated places on earth, a place that has been described as an open-air prison, a place that is expected to have been driven into nonexistence by 2020, even the daily struggle for survival is an act of resistance. The young rappers we met were creating a soundtrack of this resistance. We should all be listening.

Until It Isn't

Remi Kanazi

death becomes exciting
tolls, pictures, videos
tweeting carnage
instagramming collapse
hearts racing to break

24-hour entertainment
every glimpse, bone splinter
and shard of pain jammed
into torsos and cheekbones

loved ones want to
sit for a minute
and cry quietly

no words, no poetry
before internet and
dialed up emotions

before black and
white ideologies

before a person I
called friend defended
massacres. before the
bodies were laid to rest
before chemical weapons
haunted insides. before
refugee meant grandmother

suffering 2.0
keyboard clicks
like bombs so effortlessly
dropping. all damage
collateral. never personal
voyeurs hop on and off
like carnival rides

death becomes exciting until
it isn't. until boredom sets in
and desensitization begins
until the next ride emerges
somewhere else more
captivating

WAR REPORTS

Afterwords

Sinan Antoon

My father's warm palms shielded my ears. I could hear his blood racing in his veins. As if being chased by the bombs falling outside. My mother's lips fluttered like a terrified butterfly. She was talking to God and asking him to protect us. That's what she did the last war. And he listened. Her arms were clasped around my two sisters. Maybe God could not hear her this time. The bombing was so loud. After our house in Jabalia was destroyed we hid in the UNRWA school. But the bombs followed us there too . . .

and found us.

* * *

Mother and father lied
We didn't stay together
I walked alone for hours

They lied
There are no angels

Just people walking
Many of them children

The teacher lied too
My wounds didn't become anemones
like that poem we learned in school says

* * *

Sidu didn't lie
He was there
Just as he'd promised me
before he died
He is here
I found him
Leaning on his cane
Thinking of Jaffa
When he saw me
He spread his arms wide
Like an eagle
A tired eagle with a cane
We hugged
He kissed my eyes

* * *

—Are we going back to Jaffa, *sidu*?
—We can't
—Why?
—We are dead
—So are we in heaven, *sidu*?
—We are in Palestine, *habibi*
and Palestine is heaven

. . .

and hell

—What will we do now?

—We will wait

—Wait for what?

—For the others

. . .

to return

sidu: grandfather
habibi: my love

How Not to Talk About Gaza

Colin Dayan

One

Talking about Gaza is like talking about God. We face the ineffable. We will not name. We cannot talk about what we see. Or if we do, we are accused of lacking common sense, failing to take a realistic approach to an unmanageable problem.

What is that problem? Palestinians are the problem. Like so many others in our world today, Palestinians are labeled as "terrorists" by the powerful, so that lethal force is the rule and extreme violence — or exemplary disregard — may be directed indiscriminately against civilians and non-civilians alike. The problem is not a simple one. If we pretend it is, then we risk validating those who hold Israel to an unfair standard, or worse, who question its right to exist. But in protesting Israeli government policy, expressing horror at its brutal excesses, we risk being condemned as "anti-Semitic" or worse, as "self-hating Jews."

In December 2008, I recall sitting in the Jewish National and University Library, now renamed the National Library of Israel, across from the Knesset, Israel's Parliament, and the Israel Museum. In the courtyard I noticed a sign for the Institute for Advanced Studies. Below it there is another sign for the Center for the Study of Rationality.

I had seen the crumbled homes of East Jerusalem, the uprooted olive trees, slabs of concrete and rubble in the places that Israeli guidebooks do not include. My thoughts wandered away from West Jerusalem to places rooted in Palestinian memory even as they are erased. It's hard to imagine what the word "rationality" means in this context. Just six days later, two days after Christmas, Israel began an assault on the open-air prison that is Gaza. The delirious violence, cruelty, and indifference were justified as a *reasonable* response to Hamas rocket fire. The cohabitation of claims of reason and actual barbarity makes the lethal effects of brute force less open to criticism.

I write now during yet another assault on Gaza. The tired debates about the history of Zionism and the threat of the Palestinian national movement—or, put more bluntly, about the end of Israel and what Jonathan S. Tobin in *Commentary* (November 18, 2012) calls "a war with Palestinian Islamists with no end in sight"—ignore what is specific about more than four decades of Israeli domination in the Occupied Territories. Especially masked in these debates are the unique and various forms of violence used to control the West Bank and Gaza Strip since the eruption of the Second Palestinian Intifada in September 2000. In the name of "security," Israel has implemented something like a permanent state of emergency. Brute force coexists with, to a sometimes calamitous degree, a systematic practice of discrimination, surveillance, and disappearance. Behind the barriers—and they are everywhere—live the confined, sealed off from the zone of inclusion, the Israeli state.

Two

How to talk about the beginning of the Second Intifada, which in Arabic means a "shaking off," as in shaking the dust off your hands? On September 28, 2000, Ariel Sharon visited the Haram al-Sharif or Noble Sanctuary in the Old City of Jerusalem. During this calculated affront and brilliant provocation, he announced: "The Temple Mount is in our hands," recalling the radio broadcast from June 1967, when Israeli forces occupied the last portions of Palestinian territory not conquered in 1948. Like so much else in Israel, policy is often dictated by the approach of elections. But never without further cycles of wanton violence. The day after his visit, Israeli forces opened fire on crowds of unarmed demonstrators in the Al-Aqsa Mosque compound, killing seven and wounding more than 100. Throughout the West Bank and Gaza, Israeli forces used live ammunition against stone-throwing crowds. Five months later, on February 6, 2001, Sharon was elected prime minister of Israel. On May 18, Israel launched F-16 warplanes against Palestinian targets in Gaza for the first time.

I talk about the origin scene of the Second Intifada not to excuse the suicide attacks against Israelis that followed in the next few years, but rather to raise troubling questions about the uses of lethal force and the limits of deliberate humiliation. For Palestinians, Sharon's walk on the sacred rock of the Al-Aqsa Mosque was an unbearable transgression. What followed his provocation, in addition to armed combat, seemed to some inevitable. Israel began construction of a barrier that in effect annexed a substantial part of Palestinian territory. Though it is called a "Security Fence" or "Wall," built to respond to security concerns, such discursive obfuscation or euphemism does not hide its real purpose. In 2003, John Dugard, special rapporteur of the UN Commission on Human Rights, wrote: "The fact must be faced that what we are presently witnessing in the West Bank is a visible and clear act of territorial annexation under the guise of security."

Three

I cannot hear the sounds of the air strikes on Gaza by drones, Apaches, or F-16s or see the explosions or confront the photos and videos of the bombing as Israel expands its range of targets without asking: Is there a precedent for this wanton harm and exemption from blame?

The answer is obvious. Watching the Israeli campaign, with the casualties mounting, I remember the lack of reporting during the Gaza assault of 2008. It began two days after Christmas. One day after opening up the border to deliver humanitarian aid, Israel began bombing Gaza with F-16s, ostensibly to stop rocket fire into southern Israel. Torrents of smoke, a rain of shells, people running through a crush of metal and concrete. Women and children were killed, the innocent and the guilty. The attacks began in midday, as police cadets were graduating, women were shopping at the outdoor market, and children were leaving school.

I lived in an alternate universe that bore no relation to what was happening. As more and more civilians became targets for the excesses of violence, then foreign minister Tzipi Livni announced, "There is no humanitarian crisis." On the fourth day of the deepening and broadening scenes of carnage, the *New York Times* reported on what it called "Conflict in Gaza." Then, as now, bland language spares readers the need to confront the facts. When it comes to Israel's treatment of Palestinians, people take refuge in the comfort of euphemism. Public discourse about blatant atrocities committed against large numbers of civilians turns evasive and noncommittal when these civilians happen to be Palestinians. Cruelty and indifference are justified as a reasonable response to Hamas rocket fire.

On December 30, 2008, on the fourth day of the offensive that the Israel Defense Forces called "Operation Cast Lead," rain fell as I made my way from the American Colony Hotel in East Jerusalem to Tel Aviv airport. The taxi driver lived in Sheikh Jarrah, a neighborhood of East Jerusalem where Israeli bulldozers had just demolished a few more Palestinian homes. When I asked him whether he was for Hamas or Fatah, he answered: "I'm for my wife and children." Born in East Jerusalem (part of the Occupied Palestinian Territories), he carries the blue ID card of "permanent resident" rather than Israeli citizenship. In Sheikh Jarrah, piles of upturned earth, razor wire, trash, glass, and concrete are constant reminders to him that nothing is safe, nothing is certain. The demolition of "illegally" built houses continues. They coincide with systematic dispossession, the land expropriations that lead to Jewish settlements in the heart of Palestinian neighborhoods such as Ras al-Amud, the Mount of Olives, Silwan, and Sheikh Jarrah.

On this drive to the airport along Route 443 the Wall rose high beside me. Israelis can drive to Tel Aviv without ever actually seeing Arab towns. A first-time tourist might imagine that nothing exists between Jerusalem and Tel Aviv except this road. The $3 billion system of highways and "by-pass roads" integrate the settlement blocks into the metropolitan areas of Tel Aviv, Modi'in, and Jerusalem. But each Palestinian city, town, or village forms a broken landscape, divided into cantons that are defined in Israel's terms and with only tenuous connections one to the other.

Now, through the rain, I look at another nearly completed bridge with a new railway, another new tunnel with a blue neon entry sign, evidence of continued building in Israel proper, while Palestinian villages suffer from neglect or, worse, from demolition. Sometimes I see a minaret in the distance, as if a vision from another world, a beacon to another life lifting itself up above the concrete and barbed wire.

On that day, I left Israel for the second time in two years. I never visited until 2006, when I traveled to Jerusalem to meet my husband's family. My father, though Jewish, never wanted to go there. Born and raised in Aleppo, Syria, he still spoke Arabic, drank *arak* (Arabic for "sweat"), a sweet, distilled, anise-flavored alcoholic drink, played back-gammon, which he called "tawla," meaning table in Arabic, and chanted periodically throughout the day the muezzin's call to prayer. Everything connected to his childhood was precious to him. In Atlanta—what he called the "desert of the South"—he held fast to the memories. After the Six-Day War of 1967, he changed his name from "Dayan" to "Tawil" when Arab friends would visit. They were his lifeline to music, tawla, and good conversation. This is how I remember my father's happiness in what was, I always thought, an unhappy life.

Four

Speaking with my taxi driver, I learn something of what John Berger famously called "the stance of undefeated despair" in describing the beauty and the miracle of Palestinian life in the territories. As the driver told me: "Stories can be cruel, but they are real. They have a history."

Israel, the settlements—Ma'ale Adumim, Ariel, Modi'in Ilit, Beitar Ilit—the Occupied Territories, every site has a story to tell.

That story is told through the landscape. How do lives become expendable? Dispossessed of their homes and ancestral lands and labeled as outsiders and enemies, Palestinians are confined as nothing more than superfluity. Even if their neighborhoods remain, they are ravaged and filled with debris. Uprooted olive trees. Piled-up branches and trunks of rotting fruit trees. Slabs of concrete standing out of the ground like tombstones. Fences, walls, roadblocks, earth mounds, checkpoints, trenches—we drove through a wilderness of barriers, as if some crazy wizard had decided to get all kinds of partitions into the smallest amount of space.

Five

In 2012, and during the last Gaza assault in 2014, leaflets fall as bombs continue to hit Gaza, warning civilians to get out of the way and assuring them that they are not the objects of harm. But there is nowhere to go. In photos, the warning leaflets fall like snow. "Important announcement for the residents of the Gaza Strip," they announce. They blame Hamas for the violence and warn citizens to stay away from Hamas facilities: "For your own safety, take responsibility for yourselves and avoid being present in the vicinity of Hamas operatives and facilities and those of other terror organizations that pose a risk to your safety." A risk to safety? In the open-air prison that is Gaza, 1.7 million people are unable to move in or out. Resistance to the occupation has been met with Israel's policy of isolation and nonrecognition. Living under siege since Hamas won the Palestinian elections in January 2006 and control of the Gaza Strip in June 2007, Gazans live under the constant threat of violence—targeted killings and their "collateral damage."

"The people of Gaza don't deserve to suffer," Ehud Olmert said on the first day of the three-week assault in 2008. In other words, these excesses are not punitive. Even obedience will not make them cease. Before each new stage of that offensive, leaflets bore polite warnings addressed to "residents of the area." They repeated words that fly in the face of reality and sense: "For your own safety you are required to leave the area immediately." Leave to where? Nowhere is safe. That is the horror.

Six

In November 2012, Israel, according to its own government statistics, had carried out more than 1,350 attacks since launching the current offensive. The passion for retribution stands in for a justice as infinite as it is arbitrary. Its broad sweep calculates what is innumerable. Its generality takes all kinds of individuals into its maw. Why is Israel immune from criticism? Intrinsic to its dominion and the discriminatory nature of our ability to confront its obvious violence is the politically redemptive argument of defense: Israel needs to rebuild deterrence so no more rockets can be fired on it. Obama speaks of what is happening as the proper response of a country that has the right to defend itself.

But there are alternatives to indiscriminate slaughter, to the call "to flatten entire neighborhoods in Gaza," as Gilad Sharon, the son of Ariel Sharon, wrote in a November 18 op-ed in the *Jerusalem Post*. As many have noted, Hamas had agreed to an informal truce before Israel decided to kill Ahmed al-Jabari. Gershon Baskin, who negotiated with Hamas on the release of captured Israeli soldier Gilad Shalit, reflected on "Israel's Shortsighted Assassination" in the *New York Times* (November 16, 2012): "On the morning that he was killed, Mr. Jabari received a draft proposal for an extended cease-fire with Israel, including mechanisms that would verify intentions and ensure compliance." What, then, is the IDF retaliating for? Why deprive a population of its entire infrastructure? How, as Richard Falk asked in an interview with Amy Goodman on *Democracy Now!*, does that "produce security"?

Seven

> So I will send a fire on the wall of Gaza
> Fire that shall devour its strongholds. (Amos 1:7).

Every Israeli offensive into Gaza bears a name that delivers a message meant not only for those locked up there, but also for others in Israel and the rest of the world. What do these names tell us? "Operation Summer Rain" on June 27, 2006. "Operation Autumn Clouds" on November 1, 2006. "When clouds are full, they empty rain on the earth." So said Koheleth the preacher in Ecclesiastes. Almost lyrical, like bits of haiku, these names portend nature gone wrong: rain that does not moisten but scorches the earth; clouds that promise terror so unrelenting that no season can survive it. No more autumn. No more winter.

"Operation Cast Lead" prompted a different chain of associations. Not only the ancient Israelites in their biblical battles against Canaanites and Philistines, but a slew of other transformations. I recall the song of Moses in Exodus after the Lord saved Israel from its enemies: "You blew with your wind, the sea covered them/They sank like lead in the mighty waters." Lead, known as the "salt of Saturn" in alchemy, heralds darkness and misfortune. Bodies turned into lead, buried deep below the sea or cast into new shapes, are not molded in the image of God, but rather changed into base metals, things unnatural and ripe for ruin.

Perhaps these rituals of naming move us from the realm of actuality, the undeniable realities of experience—what we see and hear and know—into the terminology of what Kenneth Burke called the "Upward Way." As we transcend the merely empirical, respond to a higher call, our judgment is suspended. Obvious harm disappears as we enter a special realm that is closed to others. We transcend the merely empirical. We forget the piddling violations of international law. They cannot hold a proverbial candle to the newest divine sanction.

The biblical code name chosen for the Gaza attacks in 2012, two years before the most recent campaign called "Protective Edge," is in Hebrew *amud anan*, meaning not "pillar of defense," as it was translated, but actually "pillar of cloud." We can disregard the clouds of smoke from buildings burning, bombs falling, and drones firing. For the defense is God's protective cloud, the cloud that hid the children of Israel from harm during their exodus from slavery in Egypt. We join with them, protected from whatever is outside our felicitous refuge. The mistranslation doubles up on the code name's original use and transforms it. Despite what is clearly real—the obvious and asymmetrical force of arms turned against the population of Gaza—Israel's pillars of fire and smoke are recalibrated as a legitimate and necessary defense, no matter the cost.

Talking about Gaza is like talking about God.

Running Orders

Lena Khalaf Tuffaha

They call us now.
Before they drop the bombs.
The phone rings
and someone who knows my first name
calls and says in perfect Arabic
"This is David."
And in my stupor of sonic booms and glass shattering symphonies
still smashing around in my head
I think "Do I know any Davids in Gaza?"
They call us now to say
Run.
You have 58 seconds from the end of this message.
Your house is next.
They think of it as some kind of
war time courtesy.
It doesn't matter that
there is nowhere to run to.
It means nothing that the borders are closed
and your papers are worthless

and mark you only for a life sentence
in this prison by the sea
and the alleyways are narrow
and there are more human lives
packed one against the other
more than any other place on earth
Just run.
We aren't trying to kill you.
It doesn't matter that
you can't call us back to tell us
the people we claim to want aren't in your house
that there's no one here
except you and your children
who were cheering for Argentina
sharing the last loaf of bread for this week
counting candles left in case the power goes out.
It doesn't matter that you have children.
You live in the wrong place
and now is your chance to run
to nowhere.
It doesn't matter
that 58 seconds isn't long enough
to find your wedding album
or your son's favorite blanket
or your daughter's almost completed college application
or your shoes
or to gather everyone in the house.
It doesn't matter what you had planned.
It doesn't matter who you are.
Prove you're human.
Prove you stand on two legs.
Run.

They Wake Up to a Truce a Fragment

Fady Joudah

They wake up to a truce a fragment
in daylight to hike
the shipwrecks of their homes
the ships
that did not come from the sea
the sea
that ebbed as witness
against its water touching the massacre
its salt
corroding the wounds

It's summer
some dead
will house-warm their graves
with the living
who come bearing inaugural
chrysanthemum and snapdragons
and some dead will part

with ice cream
coolers of street vendors
turned morticians

Tonight
by flashlight
the living will spot
their survival unconcerned
with our kindness

Diary of a Gaza War, 2014

Najla Said

July 1

Sami Kishawi writes, "Israeli soldiers and settlers are launching heavy assaults on Palestinians in the Gaza Strip and the West Bank. Almost two dozen explosions in the Gaza Strip within the last half hour, homes demolished in the West Bank, and a child run over by a settler who has, statistically speaking, well over a 99% chance of never being held accountable for his crime. Please keep Palestine in your prayers."

I always try to be diplomatic about this stuff but sometimes I just can't. If you think that Palestinians all hate Jews and are rejoicing in the death of those three young men (Naftali Fraenkel, Gilad Shaer, Eyal Yifrah), then you are a racist. That's all I have to say. As my dad used to say, "No one has a monopoly on suffering." ANY loss of life is tragic but please, please, please STOP: Stop asking me why I have so little self-esteem when the media and the world and every one around me sits by and says that the life of a Palestinian isn't worth shit compared to the life of an

Israeli. Fuck you for condoning that by letting the media misinform the world. I don't talk about politics a lot because it hurts my heart and I don't want to hear any more roundabout rationalizations about whose life is worth more, and which deaths "matter." If you care for me then you should care that this kills my heart and spirit. No one should die; no one.

Fact: One Palestinian child has been killed by Israel every three days for the past thirteen years.

July 2

News: Sixteen-year-old Palestinian boy Mohammed Abu Khdair murdered in a "suspected revenge attack" (*Guardian*).
Here we go again.

News: The headline from the *New York Times*: "As Tear Gas Wafts Outside, Palestinian Family Mourns."

Mohammed's mother, Suha Abu Khdeir says, "We don't feel safe. They took him in front of our home."
The boy who was killed is a cousin of my dear friends Aron Kader, Jacob Stowe Kader, and Gabe Kader. You who are reading this are now two degrees away from the murdered Palestinian—a child killed in revenge.

July 4

A young boy, sixteen-year-old Palestinian American Tariq Abu Khdair from Tampa, Florida, was beaten by the Israeli police during a demonstration against the murder of his cousin. Oh and these are *American* Palestinians. So remember this when you tell me I shouldn't care so much because I am American. Please. Stand up.

News: "Palestinian kidnap victim was alive when burned," reads the headline of *Haaretz*. The autopsy showed that Abu Khdair, sixteen years old, was "alive and breathing while he was being burnt."

This is an Israeli paper. Where's the outcry? Wtf is this? My god. Dear HP, whoever you may be, help us because we have obviously got no idea what we are doing on our own.

News: Juan Cole writes, "When will Palestinians get their Fourth of July?"

Juan Cole writes, "All human beings are created equal, the founders of the United States believed. That means that Palestinians, as human beings, are also created equal. The text says *all*."

July 6

I'm going to go out on a limb and say the most arrogant thing I think I can come up with: All this stuff that is happening in the Middle East— my Dad (who died ten years ago) predicted it, and all the solutions that people are coming up with to solve the problems (bi-national Israel/ Palestine), acceptance that equality is equality, etc., are the values I was raised with and the ideas I was brought up to believe in. So if you are one of those people who likes the way I see things and is appreciative of how I embrace humanity and love (while still allowing myself the human emotions of outrage, anger, and sometimes a little too much passion) but have always felt you disagree with me on one issue, because of your own history or religion, I urge you to try to read.

I hate thinking about it too, but we kind of have to if we want to return America to being what we want it to be. The Supreme Court rulings and the Occupy Wall Street movement and the NOH8 [No Hate] campaigns and the feminist movement and all of that? This is part of the same struggle. And we play a huge part. Believe me, I really know it is annoying to think about changing the situation over there because it seems untenable and unchangeable at the same time. But the facts are simple and the reality can absolutely be changed. Let's be part of that.

July 8

Gaza is exploding again. Being exploded upon. Being expelled, expulsed: whatever the word. And the divide gets bigger, deeper, faster than ever. (Just wanted to tell you).

July 9

Tala Manassah writes, "As Palestine gets pummeled by Israeli terrorism once again, I'd like to remind those of you who are looking away of something: I am from there. This is what a Palestinian looks like. Please pay attention."

News: CNN headline, "Cousin of Slain Teen Speaks to CNN." This is my friend, the Palestinian American comedian Aron Kader. "We're not the chosen people," Aron says in one of his shows. "But we're the highly recommended people." When asked how he reacts to the death of a cousin and the beating of another, Aron talked about how the violence against Palestinians forces him to "build up a wall. It is a never-ending cycle. But this one stopped me in my tracks. It sort of pierced me."

News: "Israeli Army Says the Killing of 8 Gazan Family Members Was in Error." That's from *Haaretz.* A senior air force officer says, "There was nothing to be done. The munition was in the air and could not be diverted. Although you see [the family members] running back into the house, there was no way to divert the missile."

Oops. It was an accident; we killed an entire family.

I am part of an endangered species. That's so sad.

July 10

I have nothing to say until it stops.

In 2003, my father gave a talk at the University of Washington about the Israeli occupation and the claim of "God-given land." He says that the Zionist claim on the land is not the only claim. "It's a claim among many others." Who are these others? Canaanites, the Assyrians, the Philistines, the Babylonians, the Israelites, the Archaemenids, and the Seleucids. Arabs, he said, have "a much greater claim because they have a longer history of inhabitance, of actual residence in Palestine than the Jews did." The Jews lived in Palestine about 200 to 260 years. The Arabs have lived there for upwards of 1,192 years.

At the gym, with my headphones on, I hear the sound of a rope beating rhythmically against the floor. Someone is working out, but I think someone is firing an assault rifle. And I have a full-blown panic attack.

I am reading some terrifying tweets of pre-Army Israeli teens (that's the headline from *Mondoweiss*). Here are three:

@nopausner: I spit on you, you stinking Arabs.
@dekelderi9: We wage war so this will be our land without Arabs.
@almasulin82: Hating Arabs isn't racism. It's a commandment from God.

This makes me crack in half. This can't be what we have coming out of the mouths and fingers of the future.

July 11

I've decided to say something: If you're a Jew and you live in New York City and you keep explaining to me what Israel is doing and why, and you have no effing idea what is going on except that you're Jewish and feel threatened (which I get, believe me), then read something. Even if it is biased. If you don't know what a settlement is, and you tell me you settled the land in '48, blah, blah . . . This is not about religion. It never was. It is the simplest most straightforward thing on earth: human beings, equal rights.

News: "Palestinian Rockets: The Conversation No One Is Having." Sarah Ali, a teaching assistant at the Islamic University of Gaza, writes, "Most of us are just filled with anger. Rockets help us keep the little dignity we have, and they show Israel that bombing civilians has consequences. Peace negotiations with Israel have proved futile over and over again. Israel has only expanded its illegal settlements across the West Bank. BDS is excellent, but whether people admit it or not, it's mostly violence that works with Israel. For instance, the 2012 attack on Gaza stopped, and we got some concessions (such as an easing of restrictions on fishing and farming) because Israel asked Egypt to negotiate with Hamas to stop the rockets."

I abhor all violence. But I am also committed to the *context* of the situation.

News: Avi Shlaim, "How Israel Brought Gaza to the Brink of Humanitarian Catastrophe." He writes, "As so often in the tragic history of Palestine, the victims were blamed for their own misfortunes. Israel's propaganda machine persistently purveyed the notion that the Palestinians are terrorists, that they reject coexistence with the Jewish state, that their nationalism is little more than antisemitism, that Hamas is just a bunch of religious fanatics and that Islam is incompatible with democracy. But the simple truth is that the Palestinian people are a normal people with normal aspirations. They are no better but they are no worse than any other national group. What they aspire to, above all, is a piece of land to call their own on which to live in freedom and dignity."

Yet again written by an Israeli. One I know and have spent time with. Not that it matters who is telling the truth; just that it's being told is all that is important, but still.

July 12

Edward Said: "Remember the solidarity shown to Palestine here and everywhere . . . and remember also that there is a cause to which many people have committed themselves, difficulties and terrible obstacles notwithstanding. Why? Because it is a just cause, a noble ideal, a moral quest for equality and human rights."

July 13

News: "Did Israel Really Think Hamas Would Turn the Other Cheek?" *Haaretz.* Gideon Levy writes, "Following the kidnapping of three teen-aged Israelis in the territories and their murders, Israel wildly arrested some 500 Palestinians, including members of parliament and dozens of freed prisoners who had no connection at all to the kidnapping. The army terrorized the entire West Bank with a dragnet and mass arrests, whose declared aim was 'to crush Hamas.' A racist campaign raged on the Internet and led to a Palestinian teenager being burned alive. All this followed Israel's punitive campaign against the effort to establish a Palestinian unity government that the world was prepared to recognize, its violation of its commitment to release prisoners, a halt of the diplomatic process and a refusal to propose any alternate plan or vision. Did we really think the Palestinians would accept all this submissively, obediently, and calmly, and that peace and quiet would continue to prevail in Israel's cities?"

Gaza is a prison. A prison. Talk to me about reality.

News: "Israeli Troops Used Children as Human Shields in Gaza."

For those who regurgitate the "fact" that Hamas uses civilians as human shields, here is a report from 2009's Gaza strike. It's from Amnesty International. Which I know you all respect. And since I have to say this to make sure you don't attack me for "defending Hamas": I fucking hate Hamas. So do most of us Palestinians.

July 14

News: "Christie Slams Obama for Creating Daylight Between US and Israel."

My father and all his ancestors were born in West Jerusalem. I can't live there because I am not Jewish. Even though we never sold the house. It was taken. My mom is from Beirut, Lebanon, and all her ancestors are from there too. I can't be a citizen there either because my dad is not Lebanese. I was born with a US passport because my Palestinian grandfather immigrated here and lived here and served in the US Army before ultimately moving back to Palestine. I have only lived in NYC. I don't belong in any of the places I come from. And this is what my home country, city, elected officials expect me to do and want me to feel about the place I come from: that I should further give money to help blow them to smithereens and be outraged that we are not working harder to do so.

July 15

Peter Beinart, "Here's my question for people who support Israel's bombing campaign. Let's agree that Israel has the right of self-defense. Let's agree that Hamas bears a lot of blame for this war, and for the deaths of Palestinian civilians that result from it. But let's also agree that no matter how hard Israel tries to be precise, its missiles have killed a lot of innocent human beings. To justify that, you must believe Israel is going to gain something important from this war. What do you think that is? Given that this war will almost certainly leave Hamas in power in Gaza, and that Hamas will almost certainly rebuild the weapons infrastructure Israel is now destroying, and use it against Israel again (absent some dramatic political change), what is Israel accomplishing that's worth the death of even one Gazan child?"

Abdelfattah Abusrour: "Dear Friends, Thank you for all your worries . . . but we are happy to tell you that we are fine. We are still alive . . . and we are still human beings . . . and we are still resisting through existing on our land. Despite all these tons of bombs on Gaza by the illegal Israeli occupation, and all these human beings killed and all these houses destroyed and all the mosques and hospitals demolished. We are still fine. I will not put numbers and figures. I will not make it easy for you to reduce those innocent people killed unjustly into numbers and figures and age categories. I will not blackmail your emotions and beg for your tears . . . I will not deprive each martyr from his/her own humanity and beauty. I will not deprive each home destroyed from its privacy and specificity and its own intimate memories. The smell of the food, the joyful screams of the children and their tears, the whispers of love and the foot prints of the children running around. The smell of the freshly washed clothes hanging on a rope in front of the house or on the roof to dry in the sun.

"We are doing fine, despite the complicity of a world which lost its values, and despite the carelessness of its leaders, Arabs, Muslims or others alike as if Palestinians were aliens and as if Gaza is not worthy of even looking at. We are fine, despite this poisoned media talking about fighting terrorism and wanting to uproot Hamas from Gaza. As if collective punishment is permitted against all, as if every Palestinian is guilty by nature and it does not bother them if it is a legitimate right to resist occupation, oppression and violation by every means available, armed or non-armed.

"We are here to tell you that we are here . . . and we are fine with it . . . we have no other place, no other space, no open borders to cross, no open seas to flee, and no open air to fly . . . and even if there were those possibilities we will stay . . . because simply there is no place like home . . .

"We are here to tell you that we are fine . . . and we are thankful to all those who have shown their solidarity and demonstrated in the streets against this illegal and barbaric apartheid Israeli occupation . . . you human beings from all around the world whatever your color or ethnicity or religion is . . . Thank you sisters and brothers in humanity for standing for rights and values . . . Thanks for all those who wrote a word, who shed a tear, who shouted loud their solidarity, who made a prayer, and have a thought for all the victims of this terrorism of this illegal Israeli occupation.

"History will keep the records for the just and unjust . . . and we will remember those who stood for what is right and what is just . . . and all others we will not worry about, because they will not deserve any place in our thoughts and minds . . .

"Thank you for asking about us, thank you for your worries . . . thank you for being the human beings you are in such inhuman circumstances . . . "

July 16

Four little boys went to the Mediterranean and kicked a ball around. Now they're dead. I've gone down to the Mediterranean many times — usually a few dozen miles north but pretty much the same place. And splashed and kicked a ball and laughed and eaten watermelon and lived. It's not about me; it's about the reality of humanity. Children. Playing. Should not be killed. *Ya Falastin*, you and your people are my heart. It doesn't help, I know, but it is all I can do to undo. The terror. At least a little bit.

July 17

I am on the beach in Beirut. It is 1979; I am five. There are bombs and gunshots in the distance. Sometimes my cousins and I find bullet casings in the pool by the sea. That was my childhood. It was traumatic in many ways but I got to play and live and swim and enjoy myself because I was five. I might have been killed though, like those boys in Gaza.

July 18

Tala Manassah: "For 66 years, the Palestinian people have been terrorized by a settler-colonial apartheid state. And for 66 years they have resisted with dignity, steadfastness, resilience, and an indomitable will. Colonial rule crumbles. Terrible obstacles, and devastating loss endured and further anticipated, we will remain standing. We will not disappear. We will not be silent. We will remain standing, shoulder to shoulder with all of you struggling with us on the right side of history, demanding justice and equal rights for all people. The road has been long and full of unimaginable destruction, and it is far from over. But know this: our day WILL come. It isn't a question of if, but when. Let us keep working side by side to accelerate the road to the promised land. Free Palestine."

If you don't know who Mahmoud Darwish was, you probably don't know that for years before people like me, there have been brave and beautiful artists of resistance from Palestine. I am simply trying to follow their lead. It is no easy feat. Mahmoud's voice is irreplaceable. I was lucky enough to know him from the time I was young, but you don't need to have ever met him to know him. He was one of Palestine's most beautiful gifts to humanity. This poem is everything to me right now.

The Earth is closing on us
pushing us through the last passage
and we tear off our limbs to pass through.
The Earth is squeezing us.
I wish we were its wheat
so we could die and live again.
I wish the Earth was our mother
so she'd be kind to us.
I wish we were pictures on the rocks
for our dreams to carry as mirrors.
We saw the faces of those to be killed
by the last of us in the last defence of the soul.

We cried over their children's feast.
We saw the faces of those who will throw
our children out of the window of this last space.
Our star will hang up mirrors.
Where should we go after the last frontiers?
Where should the birds fly after the last sky?
Where should the plants sleep after the last breath of air?
We will write our names with scarlet steam.
We will cut off the hand of the song to be finished by our flesh.
We will die here, here in the last passage.
Here and here our blood will plant its olive tree.

—Mahmoud Darwish, "The Earth Is Closing on Us"

July 19

We are all Palestinians. This isn't war. This is a massacre.

July 20

News: "Massacre in Shujaiya: Dozens killed as Israel shells eastern Gaza City."

Lena Khalaf Tuffaha: "There is literally a massacre unfolding live right now in Gaza. Occupation forces, because that's what they are so let's everyone stop calling them the IDF, are targeting journalists wearing bullet-proof vests, helmets, and cars emblazoned with the word PRESS. They've killed one after his car was shot at four separate times. They are targeting ambulances of the Palestinian Medical Relief on their way to the hospital. One paramedic is now dead. Over 40 people are dead and hundreds are injured. If anyone is still thinking there is some other side to this story, they need to believe that all 1.8 million of the people facing this carnage somehow experience terror and death differently than we all do. They would have to engage in some seriously racist thinking to arrive at such a conclusion."

Shehnaz Sheikh Abdeljaber: "Called to make sure my family are doing well. Second phone call today. Here is what Asmaa (14) said [It was 6 a.m.]:

'Can you hear IT?'

There was a loud boom, constant and threatening coming from the sea as we spoke. HOW could I NOT hear it.

Yes, I hear it. My heart races and I am hoping my voice does not betray me. Fear. I start to calculate the rate at which a monster ship can dock at sea and how many blood thirsty IOF [Israeli *Offensive* Forces] soldiers can invade the neighborhood and how long it would take for them to get away, AGAIN . . . (I take a deep breath and stop the chaos in my head).

'The bombing is getting closer,' she says with a deep sigh. 'It is coming from the naval ships, they shoot from there.'

'*Allah yehmeekum, habibti*' I send her a prayer that God protect them. My fingers are numb, the phone is clenched tightly in my fist.

I tell her that she could talk to me about ANYTHING. Her feelings, her fears, anything she wants to share.

'*Kwaysa*,' I'm good, she replies. I imagine her beautiful black hair pressed against the phone with deep almond eyes glazed over in the morning.

Then she says, 'Here we are . . . we are alive.'

(Then silence as the bombs continue to cause static on the phone and echo loudly in the background.)

What do I say? How do I respond? So, I ask how everyone else is doing, She replies that everyone is ok . . . 'they are sleeping.'

How could they sleep? I think to myself. All that bombing, getting closer and closer. Then again, sleep comes to those who have not slept in DAYS. Their world has been flipped upside down. 'They have seen 4 WARS waged upon them,' I hear her mother's voice repeat in my head a feeling of pain she shared earlier on during the first phase of Israel's latest, murderous rampage.

Where they are now is considered a blessing, so I assume this type of 'quiet' is a respite.

Sleep, I tell her. Sleep my sweetheart. I will let you go back to bed, good night darling.

'Good night,' she replies and yawns a sweet yawn as another bomb goes off in the background . . . click . . ."

July 21

Things you can do for Gaza today: Have gratitude for the roof over your head, the food in your tummy, and the water you have in abundance; tell someone who is talking about the conflict that you have a Palestinian friend. And she is kind, and a pacifist, and she is not an anomaly among Palestinians.

Let me, like Barack Obama and Mark Regev, be clear: This is an unequal conflict. That does not mean that Israeli children huddling in staircases know the difference between their fear and any other fear. Their fear is legitimate and it is as valid as yours and mine. Fear is fear. And Hamas needs to stop with the rockets. No one wins here. OK. There's your "both sides." BUT GAZA is a military occupied territory. And Israel violates international laws every day and has done so for sixty plus years. And Israel has an enormous army with sophisticated weapons. The numbers and images speak for themselves. I am a child of war myself. And though I was never physically injured, I understand that there is no military solution to anything. But if everyone did stop fighting, Gaza would still be a prison for people whose only crime is being descendants of Ishmael and not Isaac. Now really. We made this all up. It's made up. We are all humans. Let's make up something happier and more beautiful and inclusive, and move on. Don't know if that even makes sense but oh well . . . I'm trying.

July 22

Nothing of import.

July 23

Is it weird that part of me thinks that Nelson Mandela's ascension to heaven was the last ingredient needed to form a solid coalition of peacemakers and justice seekers from history "up there" that has taken on the state of our miserable human existence and our horrific ways of treating others from their little cloud in the sky? I'm into it. It's fun to imagine, and it's comforting to know there's a master plan, a coup if you will, a huge movement of resistors orchestrating the world's re-ordering with their brilliant minds and a little bit of heavenly magic . . . That's my brain for you. That's also my "religion."

John Kerry says that Israel is "under siege" by Hamas. Read that once. Read it twice. Three times. It doesn't get any better. We have a problem here.

July 24

Tears for everything today.

July 25

If anyone is still confused about the Middle East, here it is again, same explanation those of us who have been following it from over here for the last sixty-six years have been saying all along:

1. It's not about religion.
2. The Holocaust was perpetrated by Western Europeans, not Arabs.
3. In the same way opposing the war in Iraq doesn't make you a bad American, criticizing the Israeli government doesn't make you a bad Jewish person or an anti-Semite.
4. The only way to move forward is to recognize and accept each other's rights to live as free human beings and figure out how to share the damn land.
5. Netanyahu needs a permanent psychological leave of absence.
6. Hamas runs Gaza the way a gang runs an inner city. Think about that and imagine what you'd do if you needed protection and had no water.
7. In light of all we talk about in America in terms of gun violence it all goes back to mental health and being human and kind and understanding one another.

I'll be here saying it for the next forty years if you need a refresher. It's really not that complicated.

July 26

I need a break.

July 27

OK wait. So like, if every country in the world that we bombed bombed us as a punishment for electing our president (say, George W. Bush) because our president bombed them and they have a right to self-defense, that's legitimate? And like it's unfortunate that we had to die but it's our fault for electing a terrorist? Just checking. Vijay Prashad taught me a phrase last week: "PEP" (Progressive Except for Palestine). Love it.

July 28

News: "Five Moments Palestinians Proved They Will Never Be Defeated."

One of them is of a girl recovering her books from her bombed house.

We are titanium . . .

July 29

Nothing good.

July 30

I am listening to Pearl Jam's "Just Breathe."

July 31

News: "UN: 'World Stands Disgraced' as Shelter for Gaza Children Is Shelled by Israel."

Pierre Krähenbühl, commissioner-general of the UN Relief and Works Agency for Palestinian Refugees, said the shelling of the Jabalia Elementary A & B Girls School was a "serious violation of international law by Israeli forces. Last night, children were killed as they slept next to their parents on the floor of a classroom in a UN-designated shelter in Gaza. Children killed in their sleep; this is an affront to all of us, a source of universal shame. Today the world stands disgraced."

DISGRACED is not a strong enough word, but it does the job.

August 1

Edward W. Said: "You cannot continue to victimize someone else just because you yourself were a victim once—there has to be a limit."

The Palestinian-Israeli conflict is only "complicated" if you have one set of moral standards for the entire world, and a completely different set for the state of Israel.

August 2

Daddy, come back—help!

August 3

News: "Netanyahu Tells US 'Not to Ever Second Guess Me Again' on Hamas."

This man must be stopped. It's atrocious.

August 4

I don't sleep very well at night these days, because when I was a little girl I was in Lebanon during the war sometimes, and I don't even think I knew what death really was, but when the shells and gunshots pierced the sky and I shivered and had my first taste of what it is to really be afraid for your life, I was traumatized. And then it happened again in 2006. You can see a million movies and still not understand what that fear is. I mean the bombs are loud and all that but the added psychological element of them being real is something you can't fathom unless you've felt it. I say this not so you feel sorry for me. I was lucky and always lived in America. My cousins and aunts and uncles and grandparents really lived the war, but I had enough of it to end up with some major anxieties and fears, and a distinct knowledge of the very specific feeling that you might die, really and truly, tomorrow. Or today, or now. And so I can't look at a picture of Gazans waiting in line for food, or think about Israeli children in staircases (yes, I do think of them too), without shaking and crying. This is the legacy of war; this is the part that keeps me awake. I almost wish I had no sense of empathy.

It's crippling. Forgive me if I sound saccharine. I am trying to just be clear about this very real thing: I want the scared little kids on the other side of the world to know I'm thinking of them and I've got them in my heart. Literally. That's all. See ya.

Gaza

Hayan Charara

Stay with me, my boy
says every night before falling
asleep. He makes it easy
for me to be sentimental.
I love that he loves a toy
elephant he named
Elefante and a girl
named Amelia who loves
that he loves running
after her. I love that he believes
the sun, like grass
and distant trains
and fish in the ocean sleep
when he sleeps. I love
that he does not know
the half of it. And tonight,
I can't help myself—
I love most all

that there will be no sirens
waking him, no warnings
to flee the house, no roof
falling upon him, which
mothers and fathers
are cheering.

Gaza Renga

Deema K. Shehabi

From the underside of the bridge
to where the Mediterranean sutures the land,
one woman bronzes her arms,

someone's limbs
tucked into the lips

of her long dress.
She says, "I saw the smoke."
"It was not the smoke of a gardenless

earth nor the hemorrhage
of parentless children."

* * *

This place is all we ever
grieve for—
in illegible dreams,

in passing hours,
the daylight sealed

from our eyes,
and nothing is ever limned:
A baby on top

of the mother's dried-up
corpse in broad daylight.

* * *

The oil-stained boot prints
on the veil
are the same ones on the wall,

and the girl whose clothes
still smell like gas is replaced

by another with a rough voice
calling out . . . for what, to whom?
Balconies, buildings,

an ambulance with no driver
settle in the back of her throat.

A Gaza Breviary

Corey Robin

1. It's Friday night in late July. There's a fundraiser for "Friends of the IDF" at a synagogue on the Upper West Side.[1] On Shabbat. Which means cessation or pause.

2. "It's all but inevitable . . . that civilians will die."[2] That's how a professor of law defends Israel's actions in Gaza.

3. "The United Nations estimates that about 80 percent of the casualties are civilians, many of them children."[3] Let's assume, for the sake of the argument, that the Israelis aren't targeting civilians. If you're getting numbers like these, does it really matter?

4. The world's greatest expert on overdoing it[4] says that Israel is overdoing it.[5]

5. One benefit of the carnage in Gaza is that it has given people who've never said a word about the carnage in Syria a reason to say a word about the carnage in Syria.

6. If only the Palestinians had revolted in April. Then everyone would be supporting this Arab Spring, amirite?

7. When it comes to opposing Israel, everyone always has a better tactic. So many better tactics: It's a wonder we haven't won yet.

8. Next time someone tells you that an academic boycott of Israeli universities is a bad idea because Israeli universities are bastions of dissent against the state . . .[6]

> Tel Aviv University is giving students who serve in the attack on Gaza one year of free tuition.

> "Tel Aviv University embraces and supports all the security forces who are working to restore quiet and security to Israel, including its students and employees called up to reserve duty," the institution says in 24 July statement on its official website . . .
>   Meanwhile, a notice circulated at Hebrew University announces a collection for goods including hygiene products, snacks and cigarettes "for the soldiers at the front according to the demand reported by the IDF [Israeli army] units."

The notice, signed by the university along with its academic staff committee and the official student union, says "we have opened collection centers on all four campuses."[7]

9. Fifty Israeli reservists write against the Israeli way of war:

> To us, the current military operation and the way militarization affects Israeli society are inseparable. In Israel, war is not merely politics by other means — it replaces politics. Israel is no longer able to think about a solution to a political conflict except in terms of physical might; no wonder it is prone to never-ending cycles of mortal violence. And when the cannons fire, no criticism may be heard.[8]

10. James Baldwin in 1979, in response to Jimmy Carter's firing of Andrew Young after Young met with the PLO at the UN:

> But the state of Israel was not created for the salvation of the Jews; it was created for the salvation of Western interests. This is what is becoming clear (I must say it was always clear to me). The Palestinians

have been paying for the British colonial policy of 'divide and rule' and for Europe's guilty Christian conscience for more than thirty years.[9]

11. Ruth Wisse writes, "Palestinian Arabs, people who breed and bleed and advertise their misery."[10] That was in 1988. Today, she is the Martin Peretz Professor of Yiddish and Professor of Comparative Literature at Harvard.

12. A group of Jews occupy the office of Friends of the IDF in NYC and read a list of the Gaza dead killed by the Israelis. There is balm in Gilead. A counterterror unit of the NYPD arrives and arrests them.[11]

13. The literal othering of Palestine: *Washington Post* subhead reads, "13 Israeli soldiers, 70 others killed."[12]

14. If Netanyahu really believes that Hamas's strategy is to amass and display "telegenically-dead Palestinians"[13] why is he obliging them with his cooperation?

15. Nicholas Kristof writes, "Hamas sometimes seems to have more support on certain college campuses in America or Europe than within Gaza."[14] In support of his claim about support for Hamas on American college campuses, Kristof links to a *Washington Post* article about the American Studies Association vote for BDS.[15] In which the word Hamas appears . . . never. Not even in the comments.

16. Say what you will about Mia Farrow, she's been tweeting and retweeting messages like this: "Tell the US to stop arming Israel."[16] And kudos to the seven other Hollywood celebrities who've spoken out on Gaza.[17] Without retracting their statements, as Rihanna did.[18]

17. The Senate passes a unanimous resolution — 100–0 — in support of Israel.[19] (Libertarian hero of the anti-imperialist right/left Rand Paul complains that the resolution isn't strong enough.)[20] Next time an opponent of BDS tells you that we should be focusing on cutting off US aid to Israel,[21] ask them how they plan to scale that 100 percent wall.

18. I get an email from a group called American Friends of the IDF Rabbinate asking for a donation to support "the necessary funding for the religious needs of the combat soldiers." After all the murder and mayhem in Gaza, I can see why the "religious needs" of these soldiers are great.

19. It's July 18. First tweet I read this morning is from the *New Republic*: "'Israel is acting strategically, not emotionally, in Gaza,' writes Leon Wieseltier."[22] Second tweet I read this morning is from Alex Kane: "Israeli military analyst: Israeli tanks 'received an order to open fire at anything that moved.'"[23] I suspect both are right.

20. A reporter at Vox tweets this: "Israel-Palestine conflict has killed 14 times more Palestinians than Israelis since 2000." David Frum responds thus: "Never enough dead Jews for some."[24]

21. Thirty-three Israeli academics condemn the bombing of Gaza.[25] That's why we're not supposed to boycott Israeli academic institutions.[26] Because of these thirty-three. The logic is almost biblical.

22. "It is not just the normal anxiety of airstrikes in a crowded city."[27] Imagine that phrase—the normal anxiety of air strikes in a crowded city—applied to Chicago or Los Angeles.

23. Gideon Levy on "our wretched Jewish state":

> The youths of the Jewish state are attacking Palestinians in the streets
> of Jerusalem, just like gentile youths used to attack Jews in the streets
> of Europe . . . The Jewish state, which Israel insists the Palestinians
> recognize, must first recognize itself.[28]

24. Israeli artist Amir Schiby commemorates the Israeli killing of four Palestinian children playing on a beach in Gaza.

Please Look Closely

Naomi Shihab Nye

Where does terror come from?

    Possibly from people who are terrified.

Why does it hurt more when the killed

    were boys on a beach?

They had the breath of the sea in their lungs.

    They were running, leaving footprints.

Does the word "innocent" have no bearing anymore?

    Depends on what you use it for.

Why can't the world see?

The world can see.

It's the people with keys to bombers who can't see.

They will win. Be on top. No more shoddy little rockets from you

second-rate folk.

Maybe they forget what it felt like to be slaughtered, collectively.

It's been going on so long they forget

what they did to begin with. How this thing got going.

Why so many ended up pressed into small hard places.

They stole the land.

Murdered grandparents. Chopped trees. Rechanneled water.

Changed the stories. Kept doing it. Said everything belonged to them.

POLITICS

Yes, I Said, "National Liberation"

Robin D. G. Kelley

You can't trust a big grip and a smile
And I slang rocks Palestinian style

"The Shipment," *Steal This Album* by The Coup

For the past thirty-five years, "Free Palestine" has been etched into my political vocabulary. In the movement circles that nurtured and trained me, "Free Palestine" rolled off the tongue as easily as "Free South Africa," "Free the Land," "A Luta Continua," "Power to the People," and the ubiquitous "El Pueblo Unido Jamás Será Vencido!" I was a sophomore in college when Israel invaded Lebanon in 1982, in order to drive out the exiled Palestine Liberation Organization (PLO). Two years later, as a first-year graduate student and chair of UCLA's African Activists Association, I invited representatives of the PLO to participate in our fifth annual conference on imperialism. We received hate mail and death threats from the Jewish Defense League, and the university administration leaned on us to withdraw the invitation. But we prevailed. I completed my doctoral dissertation in 1987, the first year of the First Intifada, and like most of my compatriots attributed Israel's willingness to participate in the Oslo negotiations to Palestinian resistance. Although Oslo proved to be a disaster and a betrayal of the PLO's founding principles, we saw the prospect of direct negotiations as a small step toward an elusive national liberation.

Yes, I said "national liberation." Liberals wished for "Peace in the Middle East." We radicals regarded the PLO as a vanguard in a global Third World struggle for self-determination traveling along a "non-capitalist road" to development. Palestine stood on the frontlines in a protracted battle against imperialism and "settler capitalism." Palestinians weren't victims—at least not in my political world. They were revolutionary combatants and, thus, *models* for those of us dedicated to Black liberation and socialism.

From our current neoliberal perch, this claim must seem completely foreign, if not absurd. But in the early 1980s, we were influenced by a group of activists/intellectuals who believed another world was possible, but only through revolution. Walter Rodney, Manning Marable, June Jordan, Ngugi wa Thiong'o, Angela Davis, Chinweizu, Cedric Robinson, Vincent Harding, Cornel West, Barbara Smith, Stuart Hall, not to mention Edward Said, Eqbal Ahmad, and Samir Amin, wrote about the ravages of racial capitalism, the violence of patriarchy, the futility of parochial politics in the face of global imperialism, and the absolute necessity to resist.[1] We were living in the last decade of the Cold War, the era that gave rise to Reaganism and Thatcherism, new imperialist wars, and new revolutions in Africa, Asia, and Latin America, from El Salvador, Haiti, and Grenada to Nicaragua and South Africa. Here in the belly of the beast, capital flight, the erosion of the welfare state, neoliberal privatization schemes, the weakening of antidiscrimination laws and policies, and a wave of police and vigilante killings struck our communities with the force of a cluster bomb. The decade, in fact, opened with police killings and nonlethal acts of police brutality emerging as a central political issue, resulting in a massive urban insurrection in Liberty City, Florida, in May of 1980. That same year witnessed the founding of the National Black United Front (NBUF) and the National Black Independent Political Party (NBIPP). Black radicals took factory jobs to reach the working classes, demanded freedom for political prisoners, threw their energies behind building a socialist Africa, continued the long tradition of community-based organizing, and participated in acts of solidarity occasionally chanting "Free Palestine."

Three decades later, in the wake of the incalculable devastation caused by Israel's latest assault on Gaza, solidarity with Palestine appears stronger than ever. In every corner of the United States, people took to the streets and to social media to condemn so-called "Operation Protective Edge," Israel's latest genocidal assault on Gaza. Palestine solidarity activists built bridges with prison abolitionists, immigrant rights activists (under the banner "Stop the War on Children From Gaza to the US/Mexico Border"), labor (in the Block the Boat demonstrations), and most spectacularly with the struggle against racist police violence in Ferguson/St. Louis, Missouri. What drives most of these acts of solidarity, however, is empathy for Palestinian suffering and/or recognition of common experiences of oppression. Spectacular violence is guaranteed to generate condemnation, which explains why outrage tends to ebb and flow with Israeli military incursions, rising precipitously during Operation Cast Lead in 2009, and again when Israeli air strikes resumed under "Operation Returning Echo" in 2012. The 2014 criminal war on Gaza has thus far produced the most casualties, the most material damage, and the greatest moral outrage. Images of infant corpses and entire families buried beneath concrete rubble generated feelings of anger and sympathy, while propaganda efforts to portray Israelis as vulnerable, terrified victims of Hamas rockets largely backfired.

Thanks to fearless journalism and relentless activism, spectacular violence in Gaza and the West Bank has swelled the ranks of the Boycott, Divestment and Sanctions (BDS) movement, largely because it offers a tangible, ethical, nonviolent strategy to challenge occupation, the slaughter of civilians, and Israel's egregious violations of international law. Even when the movement's financial impact is minimal, the educational effect has been enormous. Thanks to years of sustained, protracted debate, the public knows a lot more about the occupation, who profits from it, and the historical roots of dispossession going back to 1948.[2] During the bloody summer of 2014, I encountered more and more people in the United States openly describing Gaza as the largest open-air prison in the world, citing the fact that our taxes subsidize Israel's garrison state to the tune of 6 million dollars a day, criticizing the US for consistently vetoing UN resolutions condemning Israel's human rights abuses while violating our own Arms Export Control Act prohibiting the use of US weapons and military aid against civilians in the occupied territories. Even a few American liberals no longer see the question of Palestine as an Arab-Israeli "conflict" rooted in some ancient, irreconcilable hostility, but rather as a colonial occupation and violation of international law and human rights, subsidized by the United States.

Then in August, as the war on Gaza rose to the top of the news cycle, so did the escalation of racist police violence in the US. The killings of Eric Garner, Ezell Ford, Kajieme Powell, John Crawford III, and most significantly, Michael Brown of Ferguson, Missouri—all unarmed, all in the space of a couple of months—were immediately linked to events in Gaza. The people of Ferguson who took to the streets to decry Brown's unwarranted murder (he was on his knees with his hands up when Officer Darren Wilson fatally shot him) faced down riot police, rubber bullets, armored personnel carriers, semiautomatic weapons, and a dehumanizing policy designed to contain and silence. Activists readily drew connections between Israeli racialized state violence in the name of security and the US—from drone strikes abroad and the killing of Black men at the hands of police—and the role Israeli companies and security forces have played in arming and training US police departments. Palestinian solidarity activists issued statements about the Ferguson protests and the NYPD killing of Eric Garner, and Palestinian activists in the West Bank have put out their own solidarity statements along with advice on how best to deal with tear gas.[3]

The Gaza to Ferguson link has been revelatory in other ways. In our lexicon—especially post 9/11—cops and soldiers are heroes, and what they do is always framed as life-saving, defensive action in the name of public safety. Police occupy the streets to protect and serve the citizenry from (Black and Brown) criminals who are seen to be out of control.

This is why, in every instance, there is an effort to *depict the victim as assailant*—Trayvon Martin, Michael Brown, Darrien Hunt—the sidewalk is a weapon, their big bodies are weapons, they lunge, glare, flail their arms as evidence of threat. In Israel/Palestine, wars of pacification and annihilation are branded as efforts to neutralize the threat of terrorism. The blockade of Gaza is presented as necessary for Israel's security. People who live under occupation experience the world as victims of perpetual war. Indeed, the police department's decision to leave Mike Brown's bullet-riddled, lifeless body on the street for four and a half hours, bleeding, cold, stiff from rigor mortis, was clearly an act of collective punishment. This is the point of lynching—the public display of the tortured corpse was intended to terrorize the entire community, to punish everyone into submission, to remind others of their fate if they step out of line. Collective punishment violates the laws of war, though in this case the Geneva Conventions do not apply. Collective punishment takes other forms as well: routine stops, fines for noise ordinance violations (e.g., playing loud music), fare-hopping on St. Louis's light rail system, uncut grass or unkempt property, trespassing, wearing "saggy pants," expired driver's license or registration, "disturbing the peace," among other things. If these fines or tickets are not paid, they turn into possible jail time, making bail, losing one's car or other property, or losing one's children to social services. The criminal justice system is used to exact punishment and tribute, a kind of racial tax, on poor/working-class black people. In 2013, Ferguson's municipal court issued nearly 33,000 arrest warrants to a population of just over 21,000, generating about $2.6 million dollars in income for the municipality.[4] That same year, 92 percent of searches and 86 percent of traffic stops in Ferguson involved black people, this despite the fact that one in three whites was found carrying illegal weapons or drugs, while only one in five blacks had contraband.[5]

How do the police and the courts get away with this? By criminalizing Blackness, much the same way the Israeli state criminalizes Arab-ness. (Of course, Blackness is also criminalized in Israel, as evidenced in the treatment of African asylum-seekers in Tel Aviv, just as

Arab-ness is criminalized in the US post-9/11). In the US, *decriminalized* Blackness exists as a state of exception—i.e., by portraying the Mike Browns and Trayvon Martins of the world as the undeserving dead, by rendering them good kids, college-bound, honor students, sweet, *as if their character is the only evidence they have of their innocence.* If we really enjoyed color-blind justice, then even someone with a dozen felony convictions has a right to due process and a presumption of innocence until proven otherwise in a court of law.

We see these same principles at work in Palestine. Focusing on the killing of innocents—children, women, elderly—to the exclusion of able-bodied men (except for journalists and the like) plays into the deserving/undeserving dead binary and assumes that all men are combatants (i.e., justifiable targets) unless proven otherwise.[6] At its core, this framing automatically excludes those defending their territory, in accordance with international law, from any claims to "human rights," foreclosing any serious conversation about the justifiable right to self-defense—whether in Gaza or Ferguson. Those deserving of human rights protections, political scientist Sedef Arat-Koç wryly observes, must "present themselves in, and effectively accept, a state of pitiful, naked humanity, a child-like innocence and helplessness, a non-politico-human status, and complete dependence on the pity and charitable recognition of outsiders." She goes on to ask: "Does it mean that resistance, struggle for dignity and justice, and an aspiration for self-determination are inherently illegitimate and suspect . . . if they are exercised by Palestinians who disagree with the Western mainstream solutions to the Palestinian question?"[7]

Of course, Arat-Koç is absolutely right. Western liberals are not pacifists: They are quick to arm "rebels," so long as they are the right rebels. The innocent child, the grandmother, the widow, are the only Palestinians deserving of liberal sympathies, for they are ostensibly unburdened by political motives, even though they dream dreams of taking back their native land, recovering stolen property, enjoying the rights of citizenship and nationality, and bringing down Israel's apartheid state once and for all. But what about those dreams? Palestinian dreams? Black liberation dreams? How did we move from a solidarity firmly rooted in the commonalities of resistance to one based almost entirely on the commonalities of oppression? From a radical vision of national liberation, a dream of building a post-Zionist, post-racist world, to a solidarity rooted in shared victimization? How did we come to pitch human rights against self-determination, as if it is an either/or proposition? Are we merely struggling for a long-term ceasefire and the withdrawal of settlements in the West Bank? Are we really fighting for a détente with an apartheid, Bantustan-style "state" ruled by the Palestinian Authority? Are we really fighting for more federal oversight of police, the "demilitarization" of local law enforcement, and a return to the myriad "standard" weapons cops used to kill us in the past? Is our political imagination limited now because the Palestinian Authority is the arm of Israeli state repression rather than the governing structure of a new society? Or is it because Black political power, from the White House to the courthouse, has become the arm of US state repression rather than the leader of an authentic post-racist society?

Whatever the reasons, our solidarity ought to be based on building a new world together. I am not suggesting that we abandon the struggle to hold Israel accountable for its continued crimes against humanity and violations of international law, or that we stop mourning and honoring the dead, or that we cease any of the immediate actions designed to sustain life and bring a modicum of peace. But peace is impossible without justice. The brilliant Egyptian writer Ahdaf Soueif put it best: "The world treated Gaza as a humanitarian case, as if what the Palestinians needed was aid. What Gaza needs is freedom."[8] And what is freedom for Palestine? "Free Palestine" means, *at a minimum*, completely ending the occupation; dismantling all vestiges of apartheid and eradicating racism; holding Israel accountable for war crimes; suspending the use of administrative detention, jailing of minors, and political repression; freeing all political prisoners; recognizing the fundamental rights of all Palestinian and Bedouin citizens of Israel for full equality and nationality; ensuring all Palestinians a right to return and to receive just compensation for property and lives stolen, destroyed, and damaged in one of the greatest colonial crimes of the twentieth century.

Ironically, as AIPAC-backed, right-wing Christian Zionist organizations, such as the Vanguard Leadership Group (VLG) and Christians United for Israel (CUFI), work furiously to recruit Black students, elected officials, and religious leaders to serve as moral shields for Israel's policies of subjugation, settlement, segregation, and dispossession,[9] it was precisely the Zionist promise of a new society based on the principles of justice, liberation, and self-determination that attracted such overwhelming Black support for the founding of Israel. This is a complicated story. Black identification with Zionism predates the formation of Israel as a modern state. For over two centuries, the biblical book of "Exodus," the story of the flight of the Jews out of Egypt and the establishment of Israel, emerged as the principal political and moral compass for African Americans. "Exodus" provided Black people not only with a narrative of slavery, emancipation, and renewal, but with a language to critique America's racist state since the biblical Israel represented a new beginning.[10]

When Israel was founded in 1948, Black leaders and the Black press, for the most part, were jubilant. Few Black writers mentioned Arab dispossession, the Nakba, or the terror tactics of the Haganah. Instead, Black leaders and the Black press embraced the founding of Israel because they recognized European Jewry as an oppressed and homeless people determined to build a nation of their own. In a speech backing the partition plan, socialist labor leader A. Philip Randolph said that he could not conceive of a more "heroic and challenging struggle for human rights, justice, and freedom" than the creation of a Jewish homeland. "Because Negroes are themselves a victim of hate and persecution, oppression and outrage," he argued, "they should be the first to be willing to stand up and be counted on . . . in this fight for the right of the Jews to set up a commonwealth in Palestine."[11] And yet, in defending a Jewish homeland, Black leaders and the press often succumbed to anti-Arab racism, depicting Arabs as the brutal, bloodthirsty aggressors and the Jews as the heroic defenders of the nation and purveyors of civilization. In March 1948, the *Atlanta Daily World* ran a photo of Arab "snipers" juxtaposed to another photo of Jewish men standing guard under the caption, "Violence in the Holy Land."[12]

There were exceptions. The iconoclastic writer George Schuyler used his column in the *Pittsburgh Courier* to criticize the expulsion of the Arabs. "The same people who properly condemned and fought against German, Italian and Japanese imperialism . . . now rise to the vociferous defense of Zionist imperialism which makes the same excuse of the need for 'living space' and tries to secure it at the expense of the Arabs with military force financed and recruited from abroad." Schuyler dismissed characterizations of Arabs as "'backward,' ignorant, illiterate and incapable of properly developing the land" as thinly veiled justifications for a Jewish state, reminding his readers that this was the same argument used by the Nazis to invade Czechoslovakia, Poland, and Russia, and to justify European colonialism.[13] Schuyler was not only deluged with letters accusing him of anti-Semitism and downright lunacy, but his own paper rebuked him in an unsigned editorial.[14]

These postwar Black intellectuals and activists who viewed Israel as a model of national liberation were not dupes, nor were they acting out of some obligatory commitment to a Black-Jewish alliance. Rather, with the exception of figures such as George S. Schuyler, they failed to see Israel as a colonial project founded on the subjugation of indigenous people. Why? First, Zionism was seen in 1948 as a nationalist movement forged in the cauldron of racist/ethnic/religious oppression, resisting the post-Ottoman colonial domination of the region by Britain and France, and poised to bring modernization to a so-called backward Arab world. The nationalist and anticolonial character of Israel's war of independence camouflaged its own colonial designs.[15] Second, the Holocaust was critical, not just for the obvious reasons that the genocide generated global indignation and sympathy for the plight of Jews and justified Zionist arguments for a homeland, but because, as Aimé Césaire argued in *Discourse on Colonialism* (1950), the Holocaust itself was a manifestation of colonial violence. Israel comes into being as a nation identified as victims of colonial/racist violence, through armed insurrection against British imperialism. It is a narrative that renders invisible the Nakba—the core violence of ethnic cleansing. The myth of Israel's heroic war of liberation against the British convinced even the most anticolonial intellectuals to link Israel's independence with African independence and Third World liberation. Israel's ruling Labor Party pursued alliances with African nations under the guise that they, too, were part of the Non-Aligned Movement,[16] and Israeli leaders publicly condemned racism and presented Israel as a model democracy. In 1961, when South Africa's Prime Minister Hendrik Verwoerd tried to deflect international criticism of his country by describing Israel as "an apartheid state" ("The Jews took Israel from the Arabs after the Arabs had lived there for a thousand years."[17]), Israeli leaders promptly denounced him. Indeed, in 1963, then Foreign Minister Golda Meir told the UN General Assembly that Israelis "naturally oppose policies of apartheid, colonialism and racial or religious discrimination wherever they exist."[18]

Meir wasn't the first foreign minister to lie to the General Assembly, nor would she be the last. The Non-Aligned Movement never embraced Israel, which it had come to see as a colonial power. In 1956, Israel joined Britain and France in a joint military invasion of Egypt after President Colonel Gamal Abdel Nasser decided to nationalize the Suez Canal Company.[19] As part of the war on Egypt, Israel occupied southern Gaza and slaughtered Palestinian refugees and other civilians in Khan Yunis, Rafah, and the nearby village of Kafr Qasim.[20] Eight years later, Malcolm X visited the refugee camp at Khan Yunis during his two-month stay in Egypt and learned of the massacres, inspiring his oft-quoted essay, "Zionist Logic" which appeared in the *Egyptian Gazette*, September 17, 1964. Malcolm concluded that Zionism represented a "new form of colonialism," disguised behind biblical claims and philanthropic rhetoric, but still based on the subjugation and dispossession of indigenous people and backed by US "dollarism."[21]

The 1967 Arab-Israeli War brought many more African Americans around to Malcolm's position. The Black Caucus of Chicago's New

Politics Convention of 1967 unsuccessfully proposed a resolution condemning the "imperialist Zionist war," and the Black Panther Party followed suit, not only denouncing Israel's land grab, but pledging its support for the PLO.[22] The event that drew the most ire from liberal Zionists, many of whom had been veteran supporters of the civil rights movement, was the publication of "Third World Round-up: The Palestine Problem: Test Your Knowledge," in the Student Nonviolent Coordinating Committee (SNCC) newsletter. It described Israel as a colonial state backed by US imperialism and Palestinians as victims of racial subjugation. In short, Black identification with Zionism as a striving for land and self-determination gave way to *a radical critique of Zionism as a form of settler colonialism akin to American racism and South African apartheid.*[23]

As a result of SNCC's article, "responsible" Black leaders were called on to denounce the statement as anti-Semitic and to pledge their fealty to Israel. It was in this atmosphere that Dr. Martin Luther King Jr., made his oft-quoted statement: "We must stand with all of our might to protect [Israel's] right to exist, its territorial integrity. I see Israel, and never mind saying it, as one of the great outposts of democracy in the world." Pick up most literature from AIPAC or Stand With Us or CUFI and you will likely see this quote emblazoned in bold letters but bereft of any context. King's words come from a long, public interview conducted by Rabbi Everett Gendler at the 68th annual convention of the Rabbinical Society on March 25, 1968—ten days before his assassination and ten months after the War.[24] Revisiting it is highly instructive. First, Gendler tried to cajole him into denouncing "anti-Semitic and anti-Israel Negroes." But King pushed back. Dismissing the claim that anti-Semitism was rampant in the Black movement, he argued instead that Black-Jewish tensions stem primarily from economic inequality and exploitation. He implored the audience "to condemn injustice wherever it exists. We found injustices in the black community . . . And we condemn them. I think when we find examples of exploitation, it must be admitted. That must be done in the Jewish community too."[25] In other words, King not only insisted on condemning all forms of injustice but he refused to allow the charge of anti-Semitism to silence legitimate criticism—of Jews or of Israel.

His remarks about Israel and the Middle East are even more striking. Short of condemning war altogether, he called for "peace" above all else. For Israel "peace . . . means security," though he never specified what security meant in this context. He also addressed what he thought peace meant for the Arabs. "Peace for the Arabs means the kind of economic security that they so desperately need. These nations, as you know, are part of that third world of hunger, of disease, of illiteracy. I think that as long as these conditions exist there will be tensions, there will be the endless quest to find scapegoats."[26] On the one hand, the statement belies a surprising ignorance of the history as well as the consequences of the 1967 war. King repeats the mantra that Palestinians suffer from hunger, disease, and illiteracy because they are poor, not because they were dispossessed of their land and property and subjected to a security state that limits their mobility, employment, housing, and general welfare. King's solution?: "a Marshall Plan for the Middle East."[27] On the other hand, by situating Palestine in the "Third World," he placed it squarely within what he identified as the whirlwind of global revolution sweeping aside the old economic structures based on capitalism and colonial domination. "These are revolutionary times," he announced in his legendary speech on Vietnam a year earlier. "All over the globe men are revolting against old systems of exploitation and oppression, and out of the wounds of a frail world, new systems of justice and equality are being born . . . We in the West must support these revolutions."[28]

We can only speculate on how King's position may have changed had he lived, but given the opportunity to study the situation in the same way he had studied Vietnam, he would have been less sanguine about Israel's democratic promise or the prospect of international aid as a strategy to dislodge a colonial relationship. To be sure, his unequivocal opposition to violence, colonialism, racism, and militarism would have made him an incisive critic of Israel's current policies. He certainly would have stood in opposition to the VLG, CUFI, and the litany of lobbyists who invoke King as they do Israel's bidding. And let's be clear: King preached revolution. Distributing humanitarian aid and ending hostilities were never the endgame. The point of civil disobedience was not to keep the status quo intact, to make the regime slightly more just or fairer. The point was to overturn it. More than a regime change, King called for a revolution in values, a rejection of militarism, racism, and materialism, and the making of a new society based on community, mutuality, and love.

Not surprisingly, I found this revolutionary commitment to build a new society in Palestine. Yes, I confronted the apartheid Wall, witnessed the harassment of Palestinians passing through checkpoints, wept over piles of rubble where Palestinian homes had been demolished and their olive trees uprooted by the IDF, walked through the souk in Hebron littered with bricks and garbage and human feces dumped on Palestinian merchants by settlers, negotiated the narrow, muddy pathways separating overcrowded multistoried shacks in the refugee camps erected in the shadows of fortress-like West Bank settlements, and was overwhelmed by the level of violence, repression, and dehumanization Palestinians had to endure. But what impressed me most were the activists, the intellectuals, the youth, who spoke confidently about a liberated country, who saw the old guard leadership and the Palestinian Authority as impediments, who envisioned and debated a dozen different paths to a democratic and decolonized future. They gathered at Muwatin: the Palestinian Institute for the Study of Democracy in Ramallah; at Mada al-Carmel: the Arab Center for Applied Social Research in Haifa; and in the refugee camps in Balata, Jenin, and Bethlehem.

Bethlehem's Aida Refugee Camp is home to the Alrowwad Cultural and Theatre Society, a genuine community center and youth theater founded by director, poet, playwright, and educator Dr. Abdelfattah Abusrour, who believes theater is a "nonviolent way of saying we are human beings, we are not born with genes of hatred and violence." Having grown up in the camp, Abusrour gave up a promising career in science to devote his life to creating a "beautiful theater of resistance" aimed at releasing the creative capacity of young people to turn their stories into transformative experiences. Abusrour's play, *We Are Children of the Camp*, is something of a collaborative venture, incorporating the kids' own stories into a sweeping narrative about Palestine since 1948. The children speak from personal experience about Israeli soldiers invading the camps, shooting their parents, and then denying them access to hospitals on the other side of the wall. They long for human rights, a clean environment, freedom, a right to return to their land, and the right to know and own their history. Condensing nearly seventy years of history in the play's title song, they sing of being made refugees in their own land, of colonies built, and villages demolished. "They put us in labyrinths," they sing, "They planted hatred in us / They considered us as insects." And yet, the children onstage, like their brothers and sisters and friends whom I met laughing, riding their battered bikes along the narrow camp streets, kicking around a scraped-up soccer ball, or peppering me with questions about America, refused to become insects to be stamped out, or cauldrons of hatred. "We may have a spring," the song continues,

> Sun may rise again in our sky
> We look to Jerusalem
> Singing for freedom in our hearts.

Palestinian lives matter. Black lives matter. All lives matter. This should be self-evident. The children at the Aida Camp remind us that what matters most is struggle. Here I am not speaking only about self-defense. To struggle is to overturn the logics of a racial regime that uses security to justify dispossession, military rule, and the denial of the most basic rights. To struggle is to begin building the future in the present, to prefigure a post-apartheid/post-Zionist society. As one song from *Children of the Camp* put it: "Occupation never lasts . . . The government of injustice, vanishes with revolution."

The same vision of revolution is evident among the young activists in Ferguson, Missouri. They, too, remind us that Black struggle matters. It matters because we are still grappling with the consequences of settler colonialism, racial capitalism, and patriarchy in the US. It mattered in post-Katrina New Orleans, a key battleground in neoliberalism's unrelenting war on mostly Black, Latino, Vietnamese, and Indigenous working people, where Black organizers lead multiracial coalitions to resist the privatization of schools, hospitals, public transit, public housing, and the dismantling of public sector unions. The young people of Ferguson struggle relentlessly, not just to win justice for Mike Brown or to end police misconduct but to dismantle racism once and for all, to bring down the Empire, and to ultimately end War. As they reach out to Palestine, and Palestine reaches back to Ferguson, the potential for a new basis for solidarity is being born—one rooted in revolution.

This Is Not the University of Michigan Anymore, Huwaida

Huwaida Arraf

"What's that noise?" my mother asks on the other end of the line. It was her birthday and I had distanced myself a bit from the demonstration at Surda, in the occupied West Bank, in order to call and wish her a happy birthday before things got really out of hand and it slipped my mind to do so. "Oh nothing. Just Israeli soldiers shooting." I left out the "at us" part.

My parents left Palestine in late 1975. They hoped to start a family in a place where they were not living under Israeli military occupation or as a barely tolerated and heavily discriminated against minority within Israel. Since 1975, they have made a life for themselves in the United States, where I was born and raised. I grew up in suburban Detroit. My dad worked at General Motors and my siblings and I were pretty much all the diversity in our schools. Though we had Arab friends and cousins around, we grew up in many ways as typical Midwestern American teenagers—at least until summertime.

In the summer, my parents packed us up and took me and my siblings "back home"—we didn't call it Palestine, just home. At "home" we became part of the life of my dad's village, Mi'ilya. Mi'ilya is an all-Christian village located in what is known as the Western Galilee, within Israel's recognized borders. The village was taken over and became part of Israel when the Jewish state was declared in 1948. Whereas Jewish forces had destroyed and ethnically cleansed a number of surrounding Palestinian villages, Mi'ilya and its residents were among the few that were permitted to stay.[1] Although the Israeli occupation of southern Lebanon was in full force barely 20 kilometers to the north of the village, and later the 1987 Palestinian Intifada would erupt in the West Bank (including most prominently in my mom's hometown of Beit Sahour), our childhood summers in my grandfather's home, surrounded by my cousins and family, were almost idyllic. We traveled back home every summer until 1986, when my dad grew tired of the increasing harassment at airports from the Israeli security services. During our 1986 trip, I was old enough to be conscious of the racial discrimination practiced against Arabs; at the age of 10, I felt the humiliation of being separated and strip-searched by Israeli airport security personnel. I would not realize until later just how much of an impact these experiences had on me.

After graduating from high school, I enrolled at the University of Michigan. This was in 1994, just when the "peace process" was in its heyday. At university, I joined the Arab student association and became active in my community. But it was not Palestine that held my attention. The "peace process" derailed us. Our eyes were turned to Iraq—devastated by war and by the sanctions regime. I did not ignore Palestine though and even established an Arab-Jewish dialogue group on campus in order to create a space for contentious yet respectful political discussion.

After briefly working for an Arab American organization in Washington, DC, in the Spring of 2000, I moved to Jerusalem. By then, the "peace process" was largely a joke, with Israel repeatedly violating the terms of the agreement and the Palestinian leadership seemingly powerless to do anything about it. President Clinton had a few months left in office and there was already talk about a push for a final agreement. I wanted to be back in Palestine, so I made the decision to pack up and go.

Following the Camp David fiasco in the summer of 2000, the mood in Palestine was both angry and anxious—certainly no one had wanted to see another bad agreement made, but there was also very little indication from our leaders about what we should do as Palestinians. Every day Israeli soldiers maintained checkpoints controlling people's movement, carried out surveillance and raided villages, and arrested and held Palestinian prisoners without charge. Seizing on the opportunity that the void in the Israeli political landscape presented, hard-line Israeli opposition leader Ariel Sharon made a highly provocative visit to the al-Haram al-Sharif, the Nobel Sanctuary, which is the site of Al-Aqsa Mosque. It is also known as the Temple Mount to Jews. Palestinian Authority President Yasser Arafat is reported to have pleaded with the Israeli Prime Minister Ehud Barak not to allow Sharon to go through with the visit as Palestinians consider Sharon to have the blood of thousands on his hands from the 1982 massacres at the Sabra and Shatila refugee camps.[2] A visit by him to the holiest site in Jerusalem for Muslims, for a "political demonstration" to show "that under a Likud government [the Temple Mount] will remain under Israeli sovereignty,"[3] would inflame many and surely cause much unrest. Sharon's calculated move, designed to both provoke the Palestinians and attack Prime Minister Ehud Barak from the right, indeed sparked the Second Palestinian Intifada.

On the first Friday of the Second Intifada, I was part of the protest movement in Jerusalem. At first I wanted to see what was going to happen, how people would organize, how the spirit of the earlier Intifada would reawaken amongst the youth.

During the first few weeks, Palestinian protests were largely nonviolent. Palestinians young and old took to the streets in cities, towns, and villages throughout the West Bank and Gaza and in Palestinian communities within Israel to express frustration with *Oslo* (the one word used to summarize the entirety of the peace process). The peace process had not only failed to achieve a better outcome, but had actually worsened the Palestinian predicament by providing a smokescreen behind which Israel continued to appropriate Palestinian land and resources, expand Jewish-only colonies, demolish Palestinian homes in Jerusalem as a means of ethnically cleansing the city, and drive Palestinians into smaller and smaller areas of land from which to "negotiate" the establishment of a state.

Israeli soldiers responded to the unarmed demonstrations with lethal force, leading to the death of at least 129 Palestinians within the first month of the Intifada, including the shooting death of twelve Palestinian citizens of Israel for which no one was held accountable.[4] A combination of Israel's apparent "shoot-to-kill" policy of dealing with Palestinian protesters,[5] the impunity with which Israel operated, the widespread disinformation campaign that projected Palestinians as having had turned their backs on the peace process and resorted to violence, the distorted media coverage that blamed Palestinians for their own deaths, and a lack of trust in a Palestinian leadership that was seen as both corrupt and impotent, led to a dwindling of the popular protests and the emergence of Palestinian armed resistance. This militant resistance primarily manifested itself in the form of attacks on Israeli military installations, i.e., checkpoints, and on settlements, but also included suicide bomb attacks on Israeli buses and restaurants. It gave Israel a cover under which to indiscriminately escalate its military operations against Palestinians, employing tanks and fighter jets against a largely defenseless, occupied civilian population. As the violence, death, and destruction increased, so did the anger and the general feeling that matters were out of the hands of the people.

Even as the armed resistance took to the fore, there were still small groups of unarmed protesters trying to resist as well. When the long-time Palestinian leader and unofficial mayor of East Jerusalem Faisal Husseini died, creative street protests took place. They honored Husseini by fighting against the encroachment of Israeli control over his city. I was detained numerous times for flying a Palestinian flag in Jerusalem while protesting the shutdown of the Orient House—Husseini's former headquarters in the city, a building of historical significance to the Palestinian people. Yet, despite these efforts, to my dismay, there did not seem to be much enthusiasm for reviving the popular resistance.[6] Although I was keen to be a part of a people's uprising, I had to admit that the general sentiment was understandable. It was not that Palestinians were no longer willing to sacrifice for their freedom, but in order to sacrifice their time, resources, safety, and possibly their lives, people need to believe in the potential to achieve victory or other positive outcome. In this case, Palestinians had waged various forms of nonviolent struggle for generations to no avail. Perhaps the height of organized Palestinian nonviolent resistance came during the First Intifada, which ended or was put to an end with the 1993 signing of the Oslo Peace Accords. But those who had negotiated and signed Oslo were not representatives of the people who were in the Intifada streets—those who were beaten, injured, jailed, and killed in the 1987–93 Palestinian freedom uprising. The negotiators of Oslo were part of an exiled leadership whose control was threatened by what was happening in the streets of the Occupied Palestinian Territory, and whose fortunes had changed dramatically first with the collapse of the Soviet Union and the end of the Cold War, and then the Iraqi invasion of Kuwait and subsequent expulsion of Palestinians from the Gulf state. The net result of Oslo for Palestinians inside Palestine was more or less disastrous, and if that was what having a nonviolent uprising yielded, the thinking went; well perhaps something more drastic was required. Certainly the Israelis seemed to understand only the language of force.[7]

What would it take to convince people that we had the power to change things? In order to convince the older generation to try again, and the younger generation—most of whom only knew life under the gun—to believe in a just future, we had to inject a new dynamic, something that the Israelis could not easily target with violence and that would also change the confrontation from Israeli versus Palestinian to a global struggle against occupation and an increasingly apartheid-like situation.

During the early months of the Intifada, I had met other Palestinians and foreigners who were willing to demonstrate and who were interested in doing something bigger to support the Palestinian freedom struggle. I had heard about others engaging in ongoing, albeit limited, protests. In Beit Sahour, Palestinians and internationals marched onto an Israeli military base, on which they planted a Palestinian flag. In a small village called Hares, people chained themselves to olive trees in an effort to prevent the Israeli military from uprooting them. Eventually these various initiatives and individuals would come together to discuss how to magnify what we were doing and how to inject a new force into unarmed popular resistance. One idea was to make tangible on the ground the considerable international support and solidarity that the Palestinian cause elicited. In Durban, South Africa, at the World Summit Against Racism in 2001, tens of thousands of participants turned the event into a popular movement against Israeli occupation. In cities around the world, the start of the Intifada in September 2000 saw popular demonstrations—some numbering over 100,000—in cities across Europe, Australia, the US, Canada, Latin America, and the Middle East. Unlike virtually any other contemporary cause (that is, until the Iraq antiwar protests in 2003), the Palestinian issue mobilized ordinary people around the world to stand up and speak out.

The question to us, both as Palestinians and as activists seeking to change the balance of power on the ground, was could we manifest that solidarity into something tangible to support a people's uprising using unarmed, nonviolent tactics and strategies?

In the spring of 2001, we took the first step and sent out an email (these were the days before Facebook, Twitter, or anything called "social media" for that matter) to some groups in the US, UK, and Europe, inviting people to come to the occupied Palestinian territory to join Palestinians for two weeks of nonviolent resistance activities. With our first campaign in August 2001, the International Solidarity Movement (ISM) was officially launched. To our amazement, over fifty volunteers showed up that August, ready to participate, and more ready to go home, talk about their experiences and what they witnessed, and recruit more people. By Christmas 2001, there were hundreds of international volunteers joining organized nonviolent resistance actions throughout the

West Bank. Though the Israeli violence was escalating, and after the September 11 attacks there was a general backlash against Arabs and Muslims in the West, people continued to come and join the ISM.

What this foreign presence meant was that no longer could the Israelis simply shoot at Palestinians and claim that they were all terrorists. Now, with foreigners joining Palestinians in demonstrations, protests, and targeted actions to dismantle the checkpoints and roadblocks that were choking the life out of the Palestinian community, the picture was a new black and white—not "good guys versus terrorists," but rather, "the world against occupation, apartheid and racism." Even Israeli leftists and refuseniks starting to contact us, asking to join the ISM. The ISM became a major thorn in the side of the Israeli military, and perhaps even more importantly, the Israeli and pro-Israeli public relations machine. In late 2001, an Israeli military officer was asked what response the army would have to a massive nonviolent movement by Palestinians, and his response was honest—he said they did not have any response except to shoot.

While I was elated by the international response to the ISM call for participation, and we were seeing the reemergence of popular organizing among Palestinians, the domestic situation was still far from being a true people's uprising. The armed groups were still dominant and the political leadership continued to (mis)place its faith and confidence in world leaders rather than in its own people.

One example from that time really hit home and forced me to reconsider how much could be accomplished as long as this Palestinian leadership was in place. In the days leading up to Christmas 2001, the Israeli prime minister, Ariel Sharon, who had defeated Ehud Barak in elections earlier that year, made it clear that he would not permit Yasser Arafat to attend Christmas celebrations in Bethlehem, as he had been doing since his return to the occupied Palestinian territory in 1994. Attending midnight mass at the Church of the Nativity was an important symbolic gesture by the Palestinian leader, as it signaled the unity of the Palestinian people—whether Christian or Muslim—and helped counter unfortunate sectarian clashes that came up, albeit relatively infrequently. Looking back from today's perspective, such basic demonstration of respect and inclusion was remarkable. Sharon was seeking to deny Arafat any semblance of leadership. Palestinian officials spent the next days leading up to the Christmas mass on the phones with the Americans, Jordanians, British, French, and anyone else who would listen—including going on international satellite TV broadcasts—calling for international action to get President Arafat to Bethlehem.

For most Palestinians, this was another slap in the face, but something that was not of great concern given the ongoing human rights violations that they were suffering on a daily basis. However, as Christmas approached, more and more people expressed outrage. I then realized that between the ISM and other activist groups operating in the West Bank, we had hundreds of foreigners in Palestine who could be easily mobilized to action. I thought about Dr. Martin Luther King Jr.'s march on Washington, Gandhi's Salt March, and countless other examples of mass-based marches in the face of superior force. I called a few colleagues and we started mapping out a strategy for President Arafat to march to Bethlehem in defiance of the Israeli ban—a route that would also take him through Jerusalem on the way. With hundreds of internationals surrounding him and tens if not hundreds of thousands of Palestinians who would no doubt join the peaceful march, the Israeli military would not have a way to deal with this situation.

I called President Arafat's office, spoke to a friend I knew there, and briefed him on the idea. It was still a few days before Christmas, but time was short if we were going to make this work. He promised to get the idea to Arafat's chief advisor but explained that they were still on the phone lines with the Americans. Exasperated, I said he should ask Arafat to put his faith in his people and not George Bush. By December 24, following hours of phone calls to various Palestinian functionaries close to Arafat, I realized this was not going to happen. Disappointed by the outcome—more, perhaps, because I knew the proposal was not even brought to Arafat himself, but rather shut down by those who told us to trust them, while delivering nothing but disaster—I realized that going forward, our efforts would not necessarily be in support of our Palestinian leaders, but rather in spite of them.

Over the next years, I became involved with a number of actions and initiatives that would help shape Palestinian popular resistance, while building an international community of supporters who not only march in their own cities for Palestine, but who have experienced firsthand Israeli apartheid and thus have found more tangible action to take back home. In 2002, when Israel invaded all the Palestinian cities of the West Bank and the Palestinian leadership went into hiding, the ISM got into every city—including Jenin, where the Israelis massacred scores of Palestinian civilians in the refugee camp—and confronted the Israeli military, broke curfew to deliver food and medicine, and exposed the reality on the ground to the world. We also marched into Manger Square in Bethlehem to bring food to those trapped in the Church of the Nativity and placed foreigners both there and in President Arafat's compound in Ramallah in order to prevent Israeli snipers from indiscriminately shooting at the people besieged inside.

To deal with our unarmed, multiethnic, multinational initiative, Israel initially undertook delegitimization efforts—labeling us as "terrorist supporters" or "propaganda pawns," and later escalated to using threats and intimidation tactics against our volunteers. In 2002, long-time human rights campaigner Caiohme Butterly was shot in the leg in Jenin, seized by Israeli soldiers, and thrown at the border between Jordan and the occupied West Bank, effectively deporting her. A few months later, in March 2003, the Israeli military ran over twenty-three-year-old American volunteer Rachel Corrie with a D9 armored bulldozer in Gaza, killing her. Rachel had been standing in front of the bullet-ridden home of Dr. Samir Nasrallah, a local pharmacist, where she had been staying as a guest of the family. For two hours, the bulldozer driver played "cat and mouse" with Rachel as she pleaded with him not to demolish the home, until he seemed to lose his patience and plowed straight into her. Less than three weeks after that, Israeli soldiers shot Brian Avery, a twenty-four-year-old American citizen, in the face, causing him serious injury. Six days later, not far from where Rachel was killed, an Israeli soldier shot twenty-one-year-old British national Tom Hurndall, putting him in a coma for nine months after which he died. Tom had been helping Palestinian children to safety from Israeli gunfire when he, despite wearing the reflective vest of an unarmed volunteer, was sniped in the back of the head.

The killing of our volunteers necessitated a reassessment of our tactics and strategies. Israel had shown that it was willing to seriously injure and kill foreign nationals, thus calling into question the notion that internationals could provide protective accompaniment to nonviolent Palestinian protesters. The lack of any kind of significant backlash against Israel for its actions provided a green light for it to continue using lethal force indiscriminately. This would mean the likelihood for more injuries and deaths of ISM volunteers. Could we continue to ask people to join us under such circumstances? These issues were discussed among ISM organizers and volunteers, until it was decided that we would not give in to Israel's intimidation tactics. No one was under any illusion that the actions we were engaging in were safe or without risk, but we believed in the power of what we were doing, and were determined that we had to continue.

And we did continue, maintaining a steady stream of volunteers that came to the occupied Palestinian territory to join Palestinians in increasingly growing popular protests. However, after the spring of 2003, partially due to the negative publicity Israel garnered for killing foreign nationals, Israel severely restricted access to Gaza and, with a couple of minor exceptions, we were not able to get our volunteers in. The isolation of Gaza continued to grow, with the situation deteriorating following Israel's unilateral "disengagement" in August/September 2005. In a much heralded "pullout," Israel evacuated approximately 9,000 Jewish settlers from twenty-one illegal colonies in Gaza and redeployed its military from within the Gaza Strip to its borders. It then proclaimed that Gaza was no longer occupied. However, nothing about Israel's disengagement ended its occupation, or the isolation of Gaza. Israel continued to control Gaza by air, sea, and land, and to enforce a near-complete separation of Gaza from the West Bank, and from the rest of the world.

Under international law, the measure of whether a territory is occupied is the amount of "effective control" that a foreign power has over a territory.[8] In addition to control over Gaza's land crossings,[9] airspace, and territorial waters, the Israeli military maintains a buffer zone inside Gaza's borders, covering approximately one-third of it agricultural land, and shoots at Palestinians who enter this area. Israel controls what goods come in and out of Gaza, including food and medicine; controls Gaza's access to fuel, water and electricity; controls Gaza's economy and Gaza's population registry. As such, Israel maintains effective control over Gaza and, consequently, is still an occupying power there.

After elections for the Palestinian Legislative Council in January 2006 saw Hamas win a majority of seats, Israel imposed severe restrictions on the occupied Palestinian territory and, following internal strife in which Hamas ousted Fatah officials and took control of Gaza, increased its stranglehold, imposing a near hermetic closure on the strip. The restrictions included a ban on exports from Gaza, and a ban on imports except for humanitarian aid, which were reduced by 75 percent and the kinds of goods allowed through limited to an unpublished list.[10] According to Israeli authorities, the entrance of goods into Gaza was limited to a "humanitarian minimum," which meant only supplies considered "essential to the survival of the civilian population".[11] As such, a wide range of food items were banned, batteries, toys, certain medical supplies, schools supplies, all raw materials, and much more. Israel also cut fuel and electricity to the Gaza Strip. This policy, declared illegal collective punishment by the UN as well as human rights and humanitarian organizations, led to a severe decline in the humanitarian situation of the people in the Gaza Strip. Patients died from a lack of access to required medicine and medical care, the majority of factories shut down, unemployment rose to over 40 percent, over 80 percent of the population became food-aid dependent, and the general health and welfare of Gaza's most vulnerable increased, with a rise in the rate of anemia in children and pregnant women, as well as instances of malnutrition and stunted growth in children.[12]

*   *   *

Yet despite the reports, the statistics, the verbal condemnation of Israel's policy by humanitarian agency representatives, no one did anything to make Israel stop.

In 2008, I began working with the Free Gaza Movement, mobilizing to challenge Israel's closure of the Gaza Strip via the sea. That year we successfully sailed into Gaza's port five times in defiance of Israel's illegal blockade. After Israel launched Operation Cast Lead (December 2008–January 2009), we tried to send an emergency mission to Gaza, loading our small boat with two tons of medical supplies and fourteen volunteers, including doctors and journalists and a Cypriot member of parliament. That mission never reached Gaza as an Israeli warship violently rammed our small vessel, causing the boat to take on water and nearly sink. In 2009 we would sail twice more, each time attacked by the Israeli Navy and prevented from reaching Gaza. This caused us to reassess our strategy and give up on the idea of sending a single boat to Gaza. Instead, we built up the 2010 Freedom Flotilla, where rather than one small boat, we had seven vessels—three passenger and four cargo ships carrying over ten tons of supplies, and instead of a couple of dozen volunteers, we had nearly 700 from thirty-six different countries. In the early morning hours of May 31, 2010, the Israeli Navy launched a violent, unprovoked military assault on our flotilla, killing nine civilians (eventually a tenth would die from wounds suffered on the ship) and injuring dozens of others.

The following year, I worked with even more international groups to organize Freedom Flotilla II, asserting that we would not back down to Israel's violence, as well as worked with Palestinian youth in the West Bank to challenge Israel's racist and apartheid policies and expose the companies that supported them with a Palestinian "Freedom Ride."[13] All these efforts were geared toward supporting the Palestinian liberation struggle, providing an alternative to armed resistance, and making tangible the vast amount of international solidarity that the Palestinian cause elicits. In the early days of the Second Intifada, the most someone could do to support the Palestinian cause was go hold a sign in a demonstration or donate to a charity. Today, there has been a revolution in terms of what is possible and that is having consequences far beyond the individual action.

In 2005, a collective of Palestinian civil society groups came together and put forward a call for Boycott, Divestment and Sanctions (BDS) of Israel. The call was aimed at supporters of Palestinian freedom and put forth a new standard by which progress could be measured. Civil society was speaking clearly and loudly that smokescreens of peace talks and processes could not replace the realization of full Palestinian political and human rights, based on international law. Modeled after a similar effort that targeted the South African apartheid regime, the Palestinian call represented the best collective action effort by Palestinian civil society in more than a generation.

And the timing could not have been better. From 2001 to 2005, thousands of international solidarity activists had participated in the ISM, while even more had joined other solidarity-type groups that had cropped up. All these people had joined us in Palestine — bearing witness, breathing teargas, standing in endless lines at checkpoints, enduring Orwellian questioning by teenage Israeli soldiers, and experiencing the terror of Israeli military operations. Back in their own countries, virtually all were keen to do something to take those lessons and experiences home and challenge international complicity in the daily drumbeat of occupation. If ISM was the way that international solidarity could be made manifest on the ground in Palestine, then BDS was the way that it could achieve practical results globally.

While solidarity with the Palestinian cause was not new in 2001 when the ISM was launched, the application of that solidarity to engage in changing the dynamic of the conflict on the ground was. Whether it was joining protests against the Wall or dismantling checkpoints or planting olive trees in the West Bank or sailing ships to occupied territory, or maintaining a presence through each Israeli invasion of Gaza, we had created a new reality in which Palestinians could receive practical support directly from internationals. There was no need for the Palestinian "leadership" in this, and we did it despite its continued strategy of keeping its own people on the margins.

Today, the BDS movement is winning as artists, academics, banks, private companies, investment funds, churches, and a whole host of other institutions and individuals question the morality of continuing to support Israel directly or through structures that maintain the occupation. And it is former ISM volunteers at the core of most of the BDS groups around the world, even as ISM continues to maintain its presence in Palestine despite Israel's efforts to criminalize, terrorize, deport, injure, and kill ISM participants.

Back in May 2002, a few weeks before I was due to get married, I led a group of internationals through the empty streets of Bethlehem under curfew and siege. Our destination was Manger Square, the Church of the Nativity, and our cargo was food, water, medicine, and solidarity. This was the same place that just a few months prior I could imagine President Arafat surrounded by hundreds of thousands of Palestinians joined by internationals marching into and changing the dynamic of the Israeli-Palestinian conflict forever. As I led the group into Manger Square, having navigated around a matrix of checkpoints, all I could see were Israeli soldiers and armored vehicles. We quickly headed for the door of the church and I stood in front as others scampered in to join the Palestinians under siege inside. Afterward, I was detained and taken with the other internationals who did not enter the church, to the Bethlehem Peace Center where we were held at gunpoint.

We linked arms and sat down, refusing to obey the soldiers' orders when I heard a voice above me say, "This is not the University of Michigan anymore, Huwaida." I looked up and it took me a minute, but I recognized the officer as a former Jewish classmate with whom I had challenging but friendly political conversations in college, one who had joined my Arab-Jewish dialogue group. Now he was standing above me, in military uniform, gun slung over his shoulder, with a disturbed look on his face. He wanted to know "what happened" to me? Why I was supporting "terrorists." In return, I wanted to know why he left the United States to join a foreign army that was occupying the indigenous people of Palestine?

My former-classmate-turned-Israeli-soldier was right: It wasn't the University of Michigan anymore and there was no more room for dialogue about peace and coexistence without concrete action to end the colonial apartheid system that put me under his gun. Would he join me?

Samidoon: We Are Steadfast

Nora Barrows-Friedman

In the fall of 2011, a group of Palestinian activists in the occupied West Bank boarded Israeli settler-only buses bound for Jerusalem, in an act of civil disobedience inspired by the Freedom Rides during the civil rights movement in the United States. The six Palestinian Freedom Riders on Israeli public bus no. 148 were arrested by Israeli forces for "illegally" crossing over the green line—Israel's internationally recognized armistice line with the occupied West Bank—without Israeli-issued permits.[1] They said they aimed "to challenge Israel's apartheid policies, the ban on Palestinians' access to Jerusalem, and the overall segregated reality created by a military and settler occupation that is the cornerstone of Israel's colonial regime."[2]

The bravery of the activists exposed two corporations that profit from Israel's apartheid policies: the Israeli Egged bus company and the French multinational Veolia. Both companies operate transportation systems that serve Israel's Jewish-only settlement colonies in occupied East Jerusalem and the broader West Bank. Activists in solidarity around the world engaged in protests and direct actions targeting Veolia and Egged and calling out Israel's systems of racism, inequality, and apartheid. Legendary social justice activist and scholar Angela Davis remarked, "Palestinian Freedom Riders poised to collectively resist Israeli apartheid are inspired by the fifty-year-old legacy of US Freedom Riders, whose bold defiance of Jim Crow laws in the South helped to dismantle legal structures of racism. All those who celebrate the achievements of the Civil Rights Era should be prepared to stand in solidarity with our Palestinian sisters and brothers today."[3]

Every day, Palestinians challenge Israel's apartheid system in significant and creative ways, whether a specific campaign is organized, whether the media pays attention or not. Nour Joudah, a Palestinian American educator and writer, was denied entry and deported by Israel as she attempted to return to teach at the Friends School in Ramallah, in the West Bank, after a holiday in Jordan in early 2013. She, like countless Palestinian Americans every year, was turned away simply because of her heritage, last name, and being of the "wrong" religion.

Writing poetically in the *Electronic Intifada* after the arrests of the Palestinian Freedom Riders, Joudah highlighted the risks that both Palestinians and African Americans have taken for freedom:

> In the 1960s in the US, the saying was "We shall overcome." In Palestine, we say "Samidoon," or "We are steadfast." There is courage, perseverance, strength, and a deep sense of justice that binds rights struggles around the world. The mantra of *sumoud*, or steadfastness, that Palestinians hold dear, is difficult to adequately convey in translation, but it is not unique to them. It is a common root from which the oppressed draw inspiration and build solidarity.
>
> To those who stood against injustice in the 1960s, and who are proud of that moment in human history, the time has come to raise your voices again now—this time to demand justice for Palestinians and an end to rampant Israeli discrimination. The ride to freedom is long and ever-evolving. But it is also a ride that knows no geographical boundaries—whether in the Jim Crow South or occupied, apartheid-administered Palestine.[4]

One of the most significant themes within Palestine solidarity organizing is that of cross-movement building—creating coalitions within the historical and current intersections of different struggles. Discussions about antiracism, antisexism, immigrant justice, and oppressed peoples' liberation struggles are all amplified within the Palestine solidarity movement. As Hoda Mitwally of CUNY Law in New York City so poignantly said, "Our work has no value or purpose if we're not connecting it to other struggles."

"Solidarity with those who have shown solidarity with us"

Students involved with Palestine solidarity organizing are fully aware of, and outraged at, the heavily financed military partnership between Israel and the United States.

As the Obama administration's deportations of undocumented persons reach record levels, as the border becomes a cash cow for weapons dealers and military contractors, and as social services, health care, and education are left to waste, student activists in the US are organizing to dismantle deep structures of oppression.

"I think it's really important as solidarity activists to look in our own communities and see that what we're fighting against far away in Palestine is also targeting our communities here, and our neighbors and family members," said Gabriel Schivone, a longtime Students for Justice in Palestine (SJP) activist at the University of Arizona and a member of the national organizing committee.

Schivone has taken part in countless protests over the years, including an important direct action in October 2013 against the Obama administration's rampant detention and deportation of undocumented persons. Immigrant rights activists and members of Students for Justice in Palestine barricaded themselves at the entrance to a federal courthouse in Tucson, Arizona, where buses carrying migrant detainees pull up. Others, including Schivone and other SJP and immigrant justice activists, locked their bodies to the buses.[5]

Students for Justice in Palestine stated that the coordinated action was called to stop Operation Streamline—"the mass prosecution program that criminalizes, *en masse*, on average eighty (mostly Mexican and Central American) migrant detainees each day in Tucson." President Barack Obama has refused to halt the mass arrests and deportations of undocumented persons. In fact, under his term, the United States "has been deporting more than 1,000 people a day, and nearly 410,000 [in 2012], a record number," according to the *Washington Post*.[6]

Danya Mustafa, with the SJP chapter at the University of New Mexico, told me by phone on the day of the lockdown that "this is an important action to show solidarity with our brothers and sisters who are struggling here, whose families are being torn apart, whose livelihoods are being taken away from them." What is happening to immigrants and undocumented persons in the United States under the Obama administration and the Arizona state government "is an injustice," Mustafa added.

At SJP we know that injustice all too well, especially as Palestinians. We need to keep our families together. Community support is important. This is a direct action based on the needs of the community, and mothers, brothers, sisters, and fathers are coming out to support this action. We support it 100 percent. We want to show solidarity with those who have shown solidarity with us.[7]

This kind of cross-movement organizing is not a simple face-value, quid pro quo exchange. Rather, it is a deliberate strategy to synthesize solidarity itself and articulate the broader fight against the roots of universal injustices. Activists working on the front lines to challenge repression and inequity are inherently aware that they don't operate in isolation from other struggling communities—by strengthening each other, other struggles become their struggles too.

Schivone's work in documenting the impact of US-Mexico border policy has led him to uncover not just the political connections between the struggles of indigenous and migrant peoples in the United States and Palestine, but the militarist and capitalist connections as well. He started off by explaining that he sees the intersection in himself, personally. "I'm an embodiment of it," he added:

> My father came from a white settler background, a European immigrant from Italy. And my mother was born in Sonora, in Mexico. And when they married, my mom moved in with my dad and they got a house out of the El Hoya, which is a Chicana, Mexican-American neighborhood, or *barrio*, in Tucson. It was during "white flight," and they went to a sprawling urban new white development neighborhood. I lost half of myself through that process. I would grow up in public school not wanting to learn the language (Spanish) and rejecting half of myself.

It took some time, but with guidance from an older, politically radical sister, Schivone embraced his identity:

> For a while, when I started working with the migrant rights group *No Mas Muertes* [No More Deaths], that perspective on my family background became a [pillar of] my political life. But then I started, unconsciously, perhaps, dividing my time between both concerns— Palestine, SJP, student organizing on the one hand, and humanitarian aid and human rights work at the border on the other hand.

But he realized that there is no reason why they should be divided when there are fundamental ways that they're connected. "So I started connecting them," he said, "looking at ways that they're connected analytically and more deeply in structural forms."

One of the clearest ways the United States and Israel exemplify their shared values begins with the walls both countries have constructed to keep others out. At the US-Mexico border, which stretches from California to Texas, the US government's expanding practices of border militarization have reached unprecedented levels, and Israel has stepped in to not just share the technology it has field-tested on Palestinians, but to profit from this project as well. In March 2013, one of the two leading contractors for Israel's wall in the West Bank, an Israeli company named Elbit Systems, won its second contract—worth $145 million—to provide surveillance systems for the US Department of Homeland Security. Elbit's first contract with the US government provided 450 unmanned drones to the Arizona Border Patrol in 2004. Writing in the *Electronic Intifada*, Jimmy Johnson reported:

> The new DHS contract calls for "Integrated Fixed Tower systems" that will "assist [Border Patrol] agents in detecting, tracking, identifying and classifying items of interest" along the border. This contract largely reprises Elbit's role in the Boeing contract. Initial installations will be in Arizona.
>
> Both the US and Israeli projects affirm settler-state partitions of indigenous land: Palestinian land in the Israeli case and Tohono O'odham land in Arizona.
>
> The Tohono O'odham Nation is just one of several indigenous nations facing further partition because of US and Mexican border policies.
>
> And both projects intend to stop the movement of persons under the guise of "security."[8]

In 2011, Schivone started organizing tours to the border wall with other students from Palestinian, Jewish, white European, and Chicano backgrounds, "just observing, seeing it firsthand," he said. "And then talking about it, taking it in, discussing it, putting on conferences with students and speakers from all over the country from Palestine-oriented activism and from Chicano and human rights and border work. We put it all together and learned about each others' struggles."

Denise Rebeil works with UNIDOS (United Non-Discriminatory Individuals Demanding Our Studies) on issues related to the ban on ethnic studies. She attended the 2013 National SJP conference at Stanford University, and was eager to plug deeper into the Palestine solidarity community around the United States. She said she quickly realized the stark similarities between the two struggles. "Both people had their lands ripped from them," Rebeil remarked. "Both have to deal with white supremacy. And they always have to be on the defense. I realized those connections, which are really important."

Rebeil was a high school senior in Tucson in 2011 when the ethnic studies ban, House Bill 2281, was signed into law by Arizona Governor Jan Brewer. She had been an enthusiastic student in her Mexican American studies classes and was outraged when the state addressed its plans to cut them. The Arizona legislature ludicrously alleged that such classes supposedly promoted the overthrow of the US government and were "racist" against white people because they provided an alternative view to the European version of the colonization of the Americas. In the lead-up to the state's ban on ethnic studies, Rebeil and other students in Tucson tried desperately to get politicians to preserve this valuable educational link to the histories of Chicano/a and First Nations students.

"We were being ignored constantly," she said, with rage returning to her voice. "We went through the system, sending letters and trying to set up meetings, but nothing was working. As students, we knew our voices needed to be heard, and they weren't being heard."

On April 26, 2011, during a Tucson school board meeting at which members would vote to dismantle ethnic studies classes, Rebeil and other students chained themselves to the board members' chairs in a powerful, inspiring direct action that forced the vote to be postponed. The ban on ethnic studies ended up passing during the next school board meeting, but the motivation to keep pursuing educational justice for communities of color couldn't be quelled.

In March 2012, less than a year later, the largest Chicano/a student organization in the United States, Movimiento Estudiantil Chican@ de Aztlan (MEChA), adopted the Palestinian call for BDS during its nineteenth annual conference. The conference coincided with international observances of both Cesar Chavez Day, honoring the migrant workers' rights leader, and Land Day, when Palestinians commemorate the six

Palestinian citizens of Israel who were killed by Israeli forces during protests of ongoing land theft and settler colonization in historic Palestine.[9]

MEChA's alliance with SJP chapters all over the country has been vital to both communities. Students have long supported each other's events, marched alongside each other in protest of racist and unjust policies, and, like Schivone, have worked for justice seamlessly within both organizing spheres. Students involved with SJP linked up with MEChA to protest SB1070, Arizona's racial profiling law that was signed in 2010, and have collaborated in leading sustained protests in California against the 2013 appointment of Janet Napolitano as the president of the University of California. In her former role as the US Secretary of Homeland Security, Napolitano implemented the Obama administration's expanded deportation policies of undocumented persons.

Brooke Lober, a PhD student of gender and women's studies at the University of Arizona, said that one of the significant aspects of racist legislation in Arizona is that—although there are some local specificities to it—"it's not truly exceptional." She added: "Especially in terms of the history of the Southwest, it's been a really long-term effort by those in power to subjugate Chicanos through the prison system, through the labor force, and through school discipline and language discipline." Lober said that she brought a friend, Bay Area activist and educator Amirah Mizrahi, to the University of Arizona to talk about the Mizrahi (Arab Jewish)[10] experience and the colonization of Palestine. She added that during Mizrahi's workshop, it felt "like a Chicano-Mizrahi comparison began to get fleshed out, and it was really interesting to people."

In New Mexico, Ruben Pacheco, an economics and political science graduate at the University of New Mexico and an active member of both SJP and other social justice organizations, explained his involvement in the Palestine solidarity movement in the context of the rich history of resistance to colonialism in the state. In order to understand the struggle for Palestinians today, Pacheco said it was important to understand the resistance of indigenous peoples on the land he stands upon now, dating back to 1680 when the Pueblo Indians first revolted against the Spaniard colonists "and effectively kicked them out of New Mexico for 12 years." In 1967, Pacheco added, the same week that Israel waged war on indigenous Palestinians and Syrians, and began its occupation of the West Bank, Gaza Strip, and the Syrian Golan Heights, "a group of land grant activists attempted to reclaim ancestral land grants that were converted to national forest land in New Mexico. As Israeli tanks were advancing during the Six-Day War, national guard tanks were rolling through the mountains of northern New Mexico to prevent the Chicano activists from reclaiming their ancestral homelands." Pacheco's voice softened:

> We always talk about the different names that were given to Palestinian villages that were destroyed by Israel. Names of places have a historical connection to a people and their language. Changing a name is traumatizing to people. It erases memory. In New Mexico, the injustice runs thick, and both the Chicano and the American Indian populations have endured this type of historical trauma.

Pro-Israel groups courting marginalized communities

While students from marginalized communities continue to support each other's struggles for liberation and equality, pro-Israel lobby organizations are building public relations campaigns that seek to defend Israel from accusations of discrimination and racism. For example, Project Interchange, a program of the American Jewish Committee— which launched its own "Latino and Latin American Institute" intended to "secure support for Israel throughout the Americas, and foster favorable political alliances between Jewish and Latin American communities in the United States"— organizes "educational" delegations to Israel for members of the Latino/a, LGBTQ, and various religious communities, as well as media workers, business leaders, and politicians.[11] Other pro-Israel lobby groups such as the Anti-Defamation League are recruiting Latino/a student leaders to go on all-expense-paid trips to Israel.

Reporting for the *Electronic Intifada*, Rania Khalek and Adriana Maestas sought out former participants of an ADL trip to Israel organized for members of the Latino/a community. One participant "came away believing that the conflict is rooted in 'religion and centuries of mistrust between both sides,'" the journalists wrote. "This is a typical line in pro-Israel propaganda that erases almost seven decades of Israel's forced dispossession and displacement of Palestinians." Khalek and Maestas also noted that

> Michael Freund, the former deputy communications director for Israeli Prime Minister Benjamin Netanyahu, took to the pages of the *Jerusalem Post* to demand that Israel "launch a comprehensive and coordinated *hasbara*, or public diplomacy, campaign that makes Israel's case to Hispanics directly and *en Español*." Citing America's rapidly growing Latino electorate, Freund explained rather candidly, "the face of America is rapidly changing, and so too should Israel's *hasbara*." Israel, he said, must follow the example of Project Interchange.[12]

Groups like the ADL are "particularly worried" about the growing alliances between Palestine solidarity groups and the Latino community, writes Ali Abunimah in his book *The Battle for Justice in Palestine*. "For the ADL, Latino/a and LGBTQ individuals and groups are no more than passive recipients of Palestinian propaganda. The implication is that if any see a common interest, share similar experiences with Palestinians, or resist the use of their communities in Israeli propaganda, they have somehow been duped," Abunimah notes.[13]

Similarly, Abunimah adds that as Israel ramps up its racist treatment of African asylum-seekers—arresting and detaining thousands of people, sending them to squalid detention camps in the desert, and planning schemes of mass deportation back to countries where they face violent persecution and imminent death—Israel's propagandizing efforts to deflect criticism of such racist policies has been aimed at Black communities in the United States. As independent journalist David Sheen and author Max Blumenthal have so importantly documented during the past few years, Israeli politicians have incited violence and racist pogroms against non-Jewish Africans in Israel.[14] Government ministers such as Miri Regev have been the face of Israel's systematized racism toward non-Jewish Africans. Appointed to lead the sector that determines the state's policies affecting asylum-seekers, Regev famously called African refugees "a cancer," and then later apologized—not to Africans, but to cancer victims for comparing them to Africans.[15] Another Israeli leader, Interior Minister Eli Yishai, did not feel the need to mince words when he claimed in 2012, "most of those people arriving here are Muslims who think the country doesn't belong to us, the white man."[16]

In an important 2012 article in the online magazine *Colorlines*, reporter Seth Freed Wessler analyzed recent attempts by pro-Israel lobby groups such as AIPAC to fend off descriptions of Israel as an apartheid state and cover up its treatment of African refugees. By recruiting students from historically Black colleges and universities "as moral shields to make the case for Israeli impunity," AIPAC "is finding and developing a cadre of Black allies to declare there's no way Israel can be racist," Wessler wrote.[17]

However, African American student groups on campus are not, for the most part, falling for Israel's courtship. Time after time, divestment resolutions calling for university administrations to pull investments from companies that profit from Israel's occupation are supported by Black student unions. Black liberation groups like the Malcolm X Grassroots Movement and countless Black student unions on campuses across the United States have stood alongside Palestine solidarity activists—just as the once prominent Black Panther Party did in the 1960s and '70s.

Fighting institutionalized racism

Walking through a relative's neighborhood in Sanford, Florida, on February 26, 2012, seventeen-year-old Trayvon Martin was killed by a man who stalked and then shot him at point-blank range. For the murder of an unarmed Black teenager, Trayvon's killer was found not guilty and was released after a short trial in the summer of 2013.

Ta-Nehisi Coates, national correspondent for the *Atlantic*, put the acquittal in its proper context: "When you have a society that takes at its founding the hatred and degradation of a people, when that society inscribes that degradation in its most hallowed document, and continues to inscribe hatred in its laws and policies, it is fantastic to believe that its citizens will derive no ill messaging."[18] Coates continued, "It is painful to say this: Trayvon Martin is not a miscarriage of American justice, but American justice itself. This is not our system malfunctioning. It is our system working as intended."

Immediately after the trial, nearly forty US student Palestine solidarity organizations, along with two dozen Palestine rights groups and individuals (including myself), signed a national "Statement of Solidarity with Trayvon Martin and Victims of Racial Violence." The statement read:

> In light of the recent acquittal of George Zimmerman, Students for Justice in Palestine (SJP), Students United for Palestinian Equal Rights (SUPER), and other organizations that work to secure the rights of the Palestinian people take a firm position against the racist institutions and laws that allowed for the murderer of an unarmed teenager to walk free. SJP and SUPER are in solidarity with Trayvon Martin's family and loved ones, and with all victims of racist violence, as well as with the thousands of people who are working for racial justice in the US
>
> This trial highlights yet again that we do not live in a post-racial society, nor is our justice system colorblind. As [writer] Syreeta McFadden put it, "Only in America can a dead black boy go on trial for his own murder." Through an appeal to racist stereotypes and character assassination, Trayvon was unjustly criminalized, much like thousands of black youth, women, men, and trans* people in this country are everyday.

As people who are fighting for justice in Palestine, we understand how racism is used to justify and perpetuate an unjust system that oppresses whole populations. Our government tries to divide us by telling us that black is synonymous with "criminal" in the same way that it tries to tell us that Arab and Muslim is synonymous with "terrorist." In many ways the Black struggle coincides with the Palestinian struggle, from racial profiling, to youth incarcerations, to segregated roads, buses, housing, and education.

On top of this, a handful of the same corporations, like G4S and other prison industries are profiting off of the racist mass imprisonment of both African Americans in the US and Palestinians in the Occupied Territories.

We understand that racism did not end with the abolition of slavery, nor did it end with the defeat of Jim Crow, and as people who are fighting to end US support for the racist system of Israeli apartheid, we know that this struggle cannot move forward without challenging racism here at home.

We also must address racism within our own organizing spaces and college and universities. Advocating for human rights is incomplete without challenging institutional racism in the university. SJP and SUPER are in solidarity with the victims of racist injustice here at home and those struggling to end it, because we know that *La union hace la fuerza* (With unity there is strength).[19]

Nadine Aly of Florida Atlantic University said that although the campus SJP chapter is small, they've connected with other student groups on campus to fight local and global issues of injustice—including the kind of racism that let Trayvon's killer go free, as well as the codified US prison industrial complex. Student activists protested a contract between the university and the GEO Group, a private for-profit prison corporation with its headquarters near the campus, for naming rights to the football stadium. SJP members joined together with other social justice organizations to march, protest, and rally the community against the naming rights contract. After sustained protests and outrage, the GEO Group lost its contract bid in April 2013.

Aly explained why SJP members identified the GEO Group deal as a rallying point around Palestine. "It's important for various reasons, including being able to confront the school-to-prison pipeline industry," she said. "Students are taken out of school and put into prison [here in the US]. You find [the same system] in Palestine, where children are being taken and put into Israeli prisons, sometimes indefinitely. Their writ of habeas corpus is suspended." As human rights activists, Aly explained, members of SJP became involved in fighting both the US and Israeli prison industries.

SJP joined with the on-campus Dream Defenders movement, which pulled together Black and Latino/a students involved in social justice organizing. Dream Defenders launched after the death of Trayvon Martin and pushed for "Trayvon's Law," an effort to end racial profiling in Florida and repeal the racist Stand Your Ground law, which helped acquit Trayvon's killer. "We're also working for [US] prison divestment at the same time we're pushing for divestment from companies that profit from Israel's occupation," Aly added.

LGBTQ students fight pinkwashing

Judd Yadid, an Israeli journalist, described Tel Aviv's annual gay pride parade as an experience not to be missed if one wants to "experience Israel at its gayest, and some would say at its freest" — "From bronzed muscle-gods and elaborately decorated floats to pointed political placards and masses of rainbow flags emblazoned with the Star of David." This parade, Yadid said, is one of ten ways to "discover Israel's miraculously well-endowed LGBT scene."[20]

As part of its decade-old "Brand Israel" marketing campaign, Israel's tourism and foreign ministries have poured tens of millions of dollars into public relations and advertising strategies to promote the country as the "gay mecca" of the Middle East. This marketing campaign also promulgates Western tropes about Arab and Muslim culture: Israelis are civilized and gay-friendly while Palestinians are uncivilized and homophobic.

Humanities professor Sarah Schulman of the City College of New York at Staten Island, a writer, playwright, AIDS historian, and longtime social justice activist, wrote an op-ed in the *New York Times* admonishing Israel's marketing campaign—what activists call "pinkwashing"—while the state continues to oppress, occupy, and discriminate against Palestinians and ignore (queer and non-queer) Palestinian rights. Pinkwashing, Schulman explains, is a "deliberate strategy to conceal the continuing violations of Palestinians' human rights behind an image of modernity signified by Israeli gay life."[21]

Palestinian queer organizations inside Palestine are fighting an extraordinary battle against pinkwashing within the context of resisting Israel's broader systems of occupation and apartheid. "Being queer does not eliminate the power dynamic between the colonized and colonizer despite the best of intentions," wrote West Bank–based queer activist Ghaith Hilal of the Palestinian organization al-Qaws for Sexual and Gender Diversity in Palestinian Society, in an op-ed for the *Electronic Intifada* in 2013. "Pinkwashing strips away our voices, history and agency, telling the world that Israel knows what is best for us. By targeting pinkwashing we are reclaiming our agency, history, voices and bodies, telling the world what we want and how to support us."[22]

Student activists in the United States are organizing against Israel's pinkwashing and LGBT marketing campaigns as well. Hazim Abdullah, an SJP member at Northwestern University in Chicago, has talked with his friends about Israel's systematic discrimination against Palestinians and African asylum-seekers even as it promotes itself as a liberal "haven" for other groups including members of the LGBTQ community. "It's difficult feeling like the only person who brings up these issues outside of Palestine solidarity circles," Abdullah said. "But I really think that this intersectionality is such an important thing, and I try to apply that as much as I can to my life. I don't want to be drawn into everything, but I am. I'm queer, I'm Black, I'm low-income; so I have to be very pro- a lot of things, and anti- a lot of other things."

He continued: "I talk [to my friends in the Black community] about how African refugees are treated in south Tel Aviv . . . if you care about the African diaspora, you have to understand the fundamental inequalities within the Zionist system and what it takes for a Jewish state to exclude a population—whether it be African or Palestinian."

Abdullah also wants people to know about pinkwashing. With pinkwashing, he said, Israel is "gaining money through tourism, but they're also casting a negative light and stereotypes about Arab societies. That, in turn, creates a bias and a hatred towards Palestinians and Arabs."

Notably for Abdullah, these different issues ultimately tie together:

> Queer politics isn't just centered around gay marriage and military service. And that's something that I want to challenge a lot of people on. The event that I organized at Northwestern was called "Queer Liberation and Pinkwashing 101," and I had two queer speakers come to talk about queer liberation and its relationship to pinkwashing, and what Palestine solidarity from a queer perspective looks like.

Abdullah thought that it was an important event to hold at Northwestern, because it challenged the stratification that exists even inside the oppressed LGBTQ community, especially among white LGBTQ persons. In considering going to Israel to experience the heavily-marketed "gay haven" there, Abdullah said that members of the US LGBTQ community should be aware of what Palestinians—including queer Palestinians—face as a people occupied, displaced, and discriminated against. "I don't think that . . . going on a trip to a 'gay-friendly' country means it gives you a pass to oppress and ignore another group [the Palestinians]," he said.

Bringing workers' rights into the movement

Sarah Moawad, a Middle Eastern studies major at Harvard University, believes it's a prime moment to bring together different communities around a common cause. While Boston-area activists have rallied around Northeastern University's repression of the solidarity movement on campus, local unionized bus drivers have been in sustained protest against the French multinational Veolia for union-busting tactics. Palestine solidarity activists, including students, have joined forces with those transportation workers in protesting Boston's contracts with Veolia, citing human rights and workers' rights violations from Palestine to the United States.

Moawad explained that the Palestine Solidarity Committee at Harvard was contacted by a worker at the university, a chef who cooks Muslim students' dinners, who was involved in the protests against Veolia's union-busting practices. He reached out to the PSC and the Muslim student association, knowing that both the Palestine solidarity activists and union workers had common cause in protesting Veolia. "The fact that he knows this and reached out to the students is huge," Moawad explained. "We can't disappoint them. To have this worker-student solidarity is immense."

Shafeka Hashash of New York University is excited about her involvement in workers' rights organizing. Active in groups such as Students for Economic Justice on campus and a member of the National Federation for the Blind, Hashash tied BDS activism to the disability rights movement in the United States. "Boycott is now a strategy for the disability rights movement," she said, explaining the resistance against the shocking level of discrimination against differently-abled workers. "We started a campaign called Boycott Goodwill—the clothing store—because they pay disabled employees less than minimum wage." (The National Federation for the Blind confirmed that disabled employees at Goodwill Industries have been paid as little as $1.44 an hour.)

"In America, that's legal," Hashash added. "There are 20 regional CEOs who take in over $30 million a year. However, in Canada, they manage to pay everyone a full wage, because it's not legal in Canada to pay these minimum wages." To see the National Federation for the Blind engage in a boycott campaign, Hashash said, was empowering. "It's real, strategic action that can be implemented. And I see that the Palestine solidarity community is doing this. And it's not just them; I see disability networks who have signed on to the Boycott Goodwill campaign. It shows that this must be something if all of these human rights and disability advocacy networks are taking this approach."

Amal Ali, a history major at the University of California at Riverside, said that it's not a surprise that groups such as MEChA and other Chicano groups, African student unions, workers' rights activists, and LGBTQ groups are joining with SJP in common cause. But during the UC–Riverside divestment campaign, she was surprised at how easy it was to receive support from lesser-known student organizations. "When I was looking for student group endorsements and seeking out every random student organization I could think of that was not Hillel or [the on-campus Israel advocacy group] Highlanders for Israel, one group that I came across was the Society of Women Engineers," she recounted. "And I'm always going to remember this, because I walked into their general meeting with the intention of asking whether they would endorse our bill, thinking they would say, 'Who is she, what does she think she's doing here, we're the Society of Women Engineers, what do we have to do with this?'" Ali laughed.

> But I gave them all the facts, and made sure that I spelled it out in such a detailed way that they would know exactly what they were doing and why they should support divestment, and they didn't even have to think about it. It was the biggest shock to me. I realized it was because there are so few female engineers, and they knew about the struggle of just being any kind of minority. They felt that even though engineering may not have any ties to divestment or any kind of action like that. It just shows how strong this movement is in that you find allies in the most unexpected places.

Max Ajl, a doctoral student of developmental sociology at Cornell University, noted the importance of bringing together communities — from both expected and unexpected places — to make sure social justice demands are met. What the United States needs is a "big social movement that will hammer the system," he said.

Ajl added that solidarity with the Palestine liberation struggle doesn't matter much if activists can't widen their scope of involvement within the local communities. "There's no doing anything about Palestine without big structural reforms of the system we live in, and everything else is a delusion that people prefer, for obvious reasons, because delusions are comfortable. But they're not helpful."

Ajl and I spoke in the fall of 2013, after a group of university student senates in California had held votes on divestment bills. "Every victory is a victory, even if it's small, because it raises the bar of what's possible," he said. "It changes the field of what people believe is politically possible. And I think that's what's most important, but we do have to know that it's getting worse on the ground in Palestine, and we need much bigger victories *yesterday*."

Palestine solidarity activists on campuses are certainly doing their part to hammer a system that would otherwise prefer to separate and isolate battles for freedom and equality. To this effect, Dalia Fuleihan of Northwestern University in Chicago remarked on the enormous success Palestine solidarity groups have had in making these connections between other struggles apparent and resolute. "When you get such a broad coalition all pushing for the same thing, it isolates how small the actual powerful group in the situation really is," she said.

It highlights the absurdity of the way the general global system works—that there are just a few countries that are running the entire world. And it's the opinions of these small countries that are determining the fate of everyone else. It makes people aware that it is absurd, and it goes against the values that people especially in the West believe: democracy and power in the hands of the people.

The US Boycott of Palestine

Alex Lubin

*To the student at Birzeit University who asked me the question in 2004
that expanded my political horizons.*

I was invited to talk to your modern Arab studies class about the
United States. I took the opportunity to talk about the history of anti-
miscegenation laws in the US, the subject of my first book. I thought
the topic was important because Israel had recently passed the Citizenship and Entry into Israel law (Temporary Order 5763) that
regulates Palestinian citizenship and marriage in ways similar to US
anti-miscegenation law. I wanted to draw comparisons between US
and Israeli liberal settler colonialisms in order to better understand
the US/Israel special relationship as well as to consider the grounds
for solidarity I imagined between the Black freedom movement and
the Palestinian movement.

But then you asked the question that exposed the limitations of my
comparison.

Why, you asked, if the US and Israeli colonialisms were so similar in
their use of racial ideologies to keep subject populations in their place,
did African American civil rights leaders like W. E. B. Du Bois and Paul

Robeson, Martin Luther King Jr. and A. Philip Randolph, support and identify with Israel and not with the Palestinians? Why was the Zionist movement so influential on the American left, but the Palestinian national movement mostly ignored?

Something had been missing from my talk. In liberal settler societies like the US and Israel the political left often upholds aspects of settler nationalism, even amid the revolutionary fervor of their social movements. Hence W. E. B. Du Bois and others could be radically progressive within the West, even embracing the precepts of the Communist Party, while upholding the orientalism that underwrites Western enlightenment. In my analysis I had examined the US/Israel special relationship as a geopolitical alliance rooted to oil as well as an affective alliance built around shared understandings of settler liberalism and providential destiny. But, as your question illuminated, I had not considered the US/Israel special relationship as a powerful set of feelings and policies that either erases the existence of Palestine altogether, or that frames the Palestinians as always and already a security threat to both Israel and the US.

Ever since you asked me the question at Birzeit University in 2004 I have thought long and hard about how the question of Palestine is taken up, or disregarded, within the US public sphere, and about why the US left has been often unable to embrace the politics of Palestinian solidarity and self-determination. Perhaps one explanation lies in the realization that the US/Israel special relationship is constituted not only by diplomatic and economic relations but also by an international boycott of Palestine and Palestinian self-determination.

The US boycott

The US boycotts Palestine in the United Nations. On more than forty-four occasions since 1972 the United States has used its veto power in the United Nations to prevent passage of a resolution critical of Israel. On March 25, 1976, the US vetoed Security Council resolution

S/12022, calling on Israel to protect Muslim Holy Places in its ongoing military occupation of the West Bank. In June 1982 the US vetoed Security Council resolution S/15185, calling on Israel to withdraw from Lebanon. The massacres of Palestinian refugees in the camps of Sabra and Shatila would take place three months later. In February 1988 the US vetoed Security Council resolution S/19466, calling on Israel to recognize the applicability of the Fourth Geneva Convention, which defines the protections for civilian populations during times of war. In May 1990, the US vetoed Security Council Resolution S/21326, calling for an investigation into the murder of seven Palestinian workers. In December 2002, the US vetoed resolution S/2002/1385, condemning Israel's killing of UN employees of the World Food Program. In 2011 the US vetoed resolution S/2011/24, which condemned Israeli settlements built since 1967 as illegal under international law.

These are but a small sampling of resolutions consistent with norms of international law that the US has vetoed, often as the only nation in the Security Council offering a veto. The diplomatic impunity the US offers to Israeli violations of Palestinian human rights and international law amounts to a US boycott of Palestine and Palestinian lives.

The US also boycotts Palestine with the disproportionate amount of foreign aid it gives to the Israeli occupation. The US has given Israel $234 billion in foreign aid since 1948 (adjusted for inflation) and currently gives $3 billion annually.[1] This far surpasses the amount of aid given to any other country, and represents approximately 30 percent of the total US foreign aid budget, despite the fact that Israel has a thriving economy and comprises only .001 percent of the world's population. US aid to Israel far surpasses US aid in the region generally, and is clearly based on factors besides financial need.[2] Meanwhile, Israel's economy is rooted to the military hardware and research required for its occupation of Palestine, its arms economy, and the material support provided by Western allies like the US.[3]

US complicity

The US enables Israeli impunity in its ongoing violence in Gaza, lending support to various boycotts against Gazans. On July 16, 2014, four young cousins named Ismail, Zakaria, Ahed, and Mohamed, ranging in ages from nine to eleven, had been confined to their homes for nine days prior to going to Gaza's beach to resume their game of football. They were eager to enjoy a break in the Israeli assault on their homes. While playing football on the shores of the Mediterranean, the first of two Israeli bombs hit a fisherman's hut on the beach close to where they were playing. The boys fled but couldn't outrun the second bomb that landed nearby, mutilating their bodies, within eyesight of the hotel where an international press corps was based. Mohamed's father Ramiz, who is blind, told reporters that after he heard the news of his son's murder, "I felt as if the world had come to an end . . . I wish I had died before hearing he was dead."[4]

After Israel's bombing of Ismail, Zakaria, Ahed, and Mohamed, the *New York Times* published a story headlined, "Four Young Boys Killed Playing on Gaza Beach." But just a few hours later, the *Times* revised the headline to "Boys Drawn to Gaza Beach, and into Center of Mid-East Strife." Neither headline accurately depicts who did what to whom, but the second headline erased the news of the killing altogether and focused on "Mid-East Strife" rather than the Israeli bombing. NBC News led its reporting on the killing of the four boys with the following headline, "When Hamas Launches Rockets from Gaza, Israel Hits Back." In this telling, blame is placed at the feet of Hamas, and Israeli violence is already and inevitably understood as defensive, morally justified, and imposed by forces beyond its control.[5]

Throughout the violent killing of Palestinians in Gaza during Operation Protective Edge, and just thirteen days after Israel had sent bombs raining down on Gaza beach, killing Ismail, Zakaria, Ahed, and Mohamed, the US Senate gave unanimous support to Senate Resolution 526 condemning the United Nation's Human Rights Council, which had called for an investigation of Israeli war crimes. SR 526 also called for additional appropriations for Israel's defense forces, and an order to "replenish" Israel's Iron Dome rocket-defense system (Senate Resolution 526, 113th Congress, 2013–14). Democratic Senate Majority Leader Harry Reid called the UN Report condemning Israel's assault on Gaza "disgusting."[6]

The US provided Israel with many of the most deadly weapons used against the people of Gaza. In 2013 the US sent $196 million worth of parts for Apache Helicopters and F-16 jets. As Ken Klippenstein and Paul Gottinger reported, on the same day that US President Obama sought to broker a ceasefire in Gaza, "the State Department approved a possible $544 million sale of AIM-9x sidewinder missiles and associated support services to Israel. These missiles can be used by F-16s to hit ground targets."[7] Operation Protective Edge was an opportunity for Israel to test the US-funded Iron Dome defense system. When the US increased aid for Iron Dome in SR 526, it required Israel to purchase additional parts from the US weapons manufacturer Raytheon. Bloomberg's Tony Cappacio reported, "The Israeli government has agreed to spend more than half the funds the Pentagon provides for its Iron Dome system in the US, bolstering the political appeal of the missile-defense system in America."[8]

US sponsorship of Israel's offensive against United Nations' schools and hospitals, and of attacks across Gaza, including on the beach where the boys played football, makes the US complicit in the assault on Gaza. Richard Falk, former UN special rapporteur for Palestinian Human Rights, argued that US military aid to Israel during the Gaza offensive might violate the Arms Control Act of 1976, which requires recipients of US military weapons to use them only for self-defense. In the case of Gaza, Falk argues:

> There's no legal, political or moral argument that would uphold the claim that Israel is acting in legitimate self-defense . . . Gaza, from an international law point of view, is not a foreign state, but an occupied territory. It's not clear that you can exercise self-defense in relation to a territory that you are responsible for administering in accordance with international humanitarian law.[9]

American foreign aid, diplomatic cover, and rhetorical support for Israel contributes to a de facto boycott of Palestine and Palestinians. But this is not a boycott that merely withholds money from the Palestinian economy—although it does restrict calories entering the Gaza Strip. This isn't a boycott that attempts to change a state's behavior or policies, such as the international boycott organized against the system of South African apartheid. Instead, US sponsorship for the Israeli colonization of Palestine is a boycott that seeks to erase the very possibility of Palestine, and to reposition Israel as the victim of Palestinian terror, rather than the other way around.

Palestine does not exist

Your question, student at Birzeit, unearthed an archeological record of neglect and violent disregard that is due not merely to imperial hubris, but to the impossibility of anything else happening. In the US, the question of Palestine does not exist as a legitimate question at all. Palestine has been erased and rendered unknowable, framed, as it were, in contest with Zionism. Hence, within the US, the question of Palestine is represented by the phrase "the Israel/Palestine conflict." A conflict presumes disagreement on the part of at least two sovereign entities; it also presumes a level of symmetry that does not exist in Palestine. The US/Israel special relationship mutes the question of Palestine by positioning the Zionist narrative, a narrative rooted to Jewish suffering and security, as the only possible object of protection and defense. This is one of the reasons why antiracist social movements in the Americas—from Edward Wilmot Blyden's pan-African movement, to Marcus Garvey's United Negro Improvement Association, to Martin Luther King Jr.'s Southern Christian Leadership conference—have each identified with the Zionist movement's narrative of restorative justice rooted to national homelands. But the power of this identification has often precluded the possibility of identification with the Palestinian struggle to exist.

Writing in 1979, Edward Said argued that the Zionist narrative had overdetermined Western understanding of the question of Palestine. As a result, both Israel and its US supporters were repeatedly reacting to the wounds of the Holocaust by providing unquestioned support to the Israeli narrative of threat and security. In the process, argued Said, Palestinians had become "the equivalent of a past experience [the Holocaust] reincarnated in the form of a present threat. The result is that the Palestinians' future as a people is mortgaged to that fear, which is a disaster for them and for Jews." Said's intervention into the impossibility of Palestine in the Western imagination was to present Palestinians as "*representable*—in terms of our collective experience, our collective sense of things, our collective aspirations, above all, as a real and present (because historical) reality."[10]

And yet, more than three decades after Said's early intervention in *The Question of Palestine*, US government support for Israel and the Zionist understanding of reality endures. Hence, within the US, the question of Palestine is not regarded as within the moral continuum of the Jewish question—as a problem of racial modernity—but instead is ignored altogether, because Palestinians remain not only unknowable but also existentially impossible. Americans have boycotted Palestine and Palestinians for a long time.

The Palestinian struggle to be represented and to exist has taken many forms, employing the arts and actions of anticolonial movements across the third world. From the poetic imaginings of Mahmoud Darwish and Ghassan Kanafani to the powerful armed struggle of the Palestinian Liberation Organization, Palestinians have resisted their erasure in multiple ways. But many Americans have not even heard of these movements, which is why *The Question of Palestine*, written over thirty-five years ago, remains so relevant today.

A boycott of Israel?

But, dear student at Birzeit University who asked me the question in 2004 that expanded my political horizons, you began a movement during the year of my visit to your campus that is beginning to change how Americans view the question of Palestine. As the Israeli occupation divided Palestinian communities into tightly secured enclaves, you began to argue that life in the West Bank was similar to life under apartheid in South Africa. In the process of drawing this comparison, you transformed the question of Palestine from a national question involving statehood and sovereignty to a question of justice involving human rights. You called for a broad international boycott of Israel in order to force Israeli compliance with international law and the Geneva Conventions.

The call for the boycott followed the July 9, 2004, Advisory Opinion of the International Court of Justice (ICJ) that found Israel's separation wall to be illegal. The court ruled by a 14–1 vote, "The construction of the wall being built by Israel, the occupying Power, in the Occupied Palestinian Territory, including in and around East Jerusalem, and its associated régime, are contrary to international law."[11] Noting that Israel continued to ignore the 2004 opinion of the ICJ, in July 2005 Palestinian civil society bodies spanning unions, refugee rights associations, members of parliament, and community organizations across the Palestinian diaspora called on the international community to support a boycott of Israel that would mirror the international campaign to stop apartheid in South Africa:

> Inspired by the struggle of South Africans against apartheid and in the spirit of international solidarity, moral consistency and resistance to injustice and oppression; We, representatives of Palestinian civil society, call upon international civil society organizations and people of conscience all over the world to impose broad boycotts and implement divestment initiatives against Israel similar to those applied to South Africa in the apartheid era.[12]

The Palestinian Boycott, Divestment and Sanction's (BDS) movement has three clearly stated goals:

1. Ending [the Israeli] occupation and colonization of all Arab lands and dismantling the Wall;

2. Recognizing the fundamental rights of the Arab Palestinian citizens of Israel to full equality; and

3. Respecting, protecting and promoting the rights of Palestinian refugees to return to their homes and properties as stipulated in UN resolution 194.[13]

The BDS movement employs international law and human rights to hold Israel accountable for its occupation. In this way, BDS is one among many strategies working toward decolonization and national liberation.

The Palestinian BDS movement has made starkly visible the ongoing US boycott of Palestinian lives, and asks Americans to realign their boycott with a commitment to justice. At a time when governments and international agencies have failed the Palestinian people, the boycott movement asks the international community to consider whether they support the Israeli boycott of Palestinian lives, or whether they embrace the norms of international law and human rights.

You, the student at Birzeit University in 2004 who asked the question that expanded my political horizons, illuminated the absence/presence of Palestine in Western liberal discourse, while also showing me how as a professor I had a responsibility to engage in the BDS movement. Indeed, academia is one of the battlegrounds in what Ali Abunimah has termed "the battle for justice in Palestine."[14] At Birzeit University, students like you have been held in administrative detention by the Israeli occupying army, while faculty members and students with foreign passports have been denied entry into the West Bank. In 2006 the Arabic language program at Birzeit saw attendance drop by 50 percent due to the inability of foreign passport holders to enter the West Bank.[15]

While scholars in the West struggle to maintain the privileges of academic freedom amid the downsizing of higher education, Palestinian students struggle for the right to an education. In a 2008 petition to the United Nations Human Rights Council (UNHRC), the Palestinian

Right to Education Campaign outlined several ways that apartheid conditions structure Palestinian students' experiences. Palestinian detainees in prisons are denied access to education, unlike their Israeli counterparts. Israel's separation barrier blocks student and faculty travel to certain West Bank Universities. Students attending An Najah University in Nablus are regularly late to class due to checkpoints, at which they are often verbally abused. Israel prevents the formation of student groups affiliated with political parties, effectively criminalizing Palestinian academic freedom. The occupation prevents physical mobility across Palestinian and Israeli institutions, between Palestinian institutions, and internationally. Such restrictions of movement severely undermine the ability of Palestinian scholars to reach international audiences and to conduct research. And finally, the report notes the ways that Palestinian students are particularly targeted for arrest by the Israel Defense Forces.[16]

But it's not just the occupation of the West Bank that impacts Palestinians' rights to education; within Israel universities play an important part in creating an apartheid system. A 2009 report authored by the Alternative Information Center (AIC) demonstrates several ways in which Israeli institutions of higher education are complicit in the degradation of Palestinian lives. The report notes that Israeli educational institutions have provided the knowledge required to advance surveillance technologies that aid the occupation, especially during a time when fewer Israelis volunteer for the military. "The Technion, the Israeli institution most renowned for applied sciences such as engineering and computer science, has all but enlisted itself in the military."[17] Moreover, Israeli institutions discriminate against Palestinian students through a system that financially rewards current and former soldiers who attend higher education institutions. At Haifa University Palestinian students are prevented from living in subsidized on-campus housing. Israeli higher education is also part of the occupation, as witnessed by the building of the Bar Ilan University campus in the West Bank settlement of Ariel. Hebrew University is extending its campus onto the green line, while expropriating Palestinian land. Tel Aviv University is built atop the destroyed Palestinian village of Al-Sheikh Muwanis. And finally, the report documents the silencing of any dissent on Israeli campus.

But conditions have only gotten worse since the 2008 report. Repeated assaults on Gaza have decimated its institutions of higher education. In 2014, Operation Protective Edge targeted and destroyed the Islamic University of Gaza, Gaza's largest university. There is, in effect, a boycott on Palestinian education in which the US is complicit through its partnerships with Israeli institutions, including a planned joint campus of Cornell University and the Technion.

Given the major role of the US in obstructing justice for Palestine it is understandable that the American Studies Association (ASA), an academic association founded in 1951 for the interdisciplinary study of American culture and history, endorses an academic boycott of Israeli higher education. Although the ASA invites both Israeli and Palestinian scholars to its conferences—indeed there were several Israeli participants at the 2014 conference—it is committed to not establishing institutional relationships with Israeli institutions. While the boycott is largely symbolic, the ASA is a scholarly field that recognizes the material implications of symbolic politics. As the preeminent American studies scholar George Lipsitz argues, "academic struggles over meaning are always connected in crucial ways to social movement struggles over resources and power."[18] Hence, the ASA's boycott reframes the question of Palestine in the United States to address the absence of Palestine from the moral horizons of the US left, and demands a new identification with the struggle for justice in Palestine. The BDS movement is an attempt to gain representation, to cite Said again, amid the regular erasure of Palestinian lives evidenced by the de facto US boycott of Palestine. There are those who argue that American studies scholars have no place in entering the field of Middle East politics, but if our discipline is to have any relevance it must engage the US boycott of Palestine and the material implications of US support for Israel.

Boycotts require that we question with whom and with what we stand in solidarity. In the struggle for justice in Palestine, the choice for Americans is rather clear. Either they continue their decades-long boycott of Palestinians, or they choose to join the human rights struggle for Palestine and with Palestinians.

The Collapse of the Pro-Israel Consensus

Alex Kane

In October 2014, Cambridge, Massachusetts, offered a ground-level look at how the American Jewish community was changing. Harvard, one of the country's most prestigious universities, hosted the Open Hillel conference, a gathering of young American Jews fed up with dogmatic Zionism and pro-Israel censorship.

Hillel is the central institution for Jewish life on college campuses around the country, where young Jews gather for Shabbat dinners, for prayer, and for holidays. It is also an institution where supporting the state of Israel is seen as an obligation.

It was Harvard's Hillel chapter that planted the seeds for the Open Hillel conference. In 2012, the organization barred two anti-occupation activists from speaking under its roof because their event was to be sponsored by a campus group called the Palestine Solidarity Committee. In response, a small group of Jewish students launched a movement to "open" Hillel, with the goal of changing Hillel's "standards of partnership," an innocuous term for a policy of censorship. The standards deem off-limits any person or organization that, like the Palestine Solidarity

Committee, supports the Boycott, Divestment and Sanctions (BDS) movement. They also bar speakers and events that "demonize" Israel or "deny" its right to exist as a "democratic and Jewish state." In practice, the standards tell Jewish students who they can partner or work with if they want Hillel's financial and institutional support.

The Open Hillel conference showcased the growth of a network that has spread nationwide. Hundreds of students, most of them young Jews, converged on Harvard to openly discuss and debate Israel, Palestine, BDS, and Zionism. No consensus on these issues emerged, but consensus was not the goal. The goal was open conversation.

On the one hand, that such a goal is deemed threatening to Hillel and its donor base encapsulates how out of touch the older generation of Jewish leaders in the US is with young Jews' questioning, critical spirit. Open Hillel is not a radical group. They just want to speak about Israel, warts and all, freely. Hillel, however, is afraid that opening the conversation will allow critics of Israel to gain a foothold in established Jewish spaces. Yet telling young people how to think is a losing proposition, especially in an age of social media and college activism, where pro-Palestinian views are disseminated widely.

On the other hand, Hillel's fear is grounded in something real. In recent years, more and more American Jews have begun to voice skepticism about Israel's current path of occupation and colonization, as well as its periodic assaults on Gaza, which maim and kill thousands of Palestinians. The leading communal institutions have tried to enforce a pro-Israel orthodoxy for decades, and it has largely worked. But in the face of ever more Israeli atrocities and the increasing international activism they spark, the Jewish communal consensus on Israel is cracking. If it fully shatters, as it is bound to eventually, it will have a profound impact on the discourse on Israel in this country.

Skepticism of Israeli policy burst out into the open in a new way when Israel launched its assault on the Gaza Strip in the summer of 2014. The third bombardment of Gaza in five years had wide support in Israeli Jewish society, but among American Jews it polarized an already divided community. Left-leaning Jews were propelled to action against the assault, while the right followed Israeli society's lead, marching to the beat of war drums against a besieged, ghettoized Palestinian population. The groundswell of support for the Palestinian point of view has worried Jewish leaders. On August 1, Andy Bachman, a prominent liberal Reform rabbi in Brooklyn, blogged from Israel that he worried "about American Jewry on this trip more than I ever have. I worry about their increasing alienation from the notion of a Jewish people, each of us inherently obligated to one another despite our differences; I worry about our understandable abhorrence of the killing of innocents that too quickly shifts to blame, guilt and distance from Israel."

Bachman is fretting about a real trend that is exemplified in spaces like the Open Hillel conference. Speaking on stage at the gathering, Rebecca Vilkomerson, the executive director of Jewish Voice for Peace (JVP), related a telling anecdote. In the midst of Israel's military operation, a rabbi emailed her a one line message: "Enough. Sign me up." This was how a sizable portion of Jews felt as they watched their Twitter streams and the news media broadcast events like the Israeli army's killing of four Palestinian boys on a Gaza beach. Many of these Jews consider themselves a part of the American left. Some of them were disengaged from the question of Israel/Palestine because they feared breaking communal red lines, or because Israel was so divisive that it impeded other progressive work. The Gaza assault pushed many of these people off the fence.

Jewish Voice for Peace is emblematic of the way the collapse of the pro-Israel consensus has become visible since the summer. Founded in 1996, the group aims to generate action in the US toward a just peace in Israel/Palestine—a peace that, crucially, includes the rights of Palestinian refugees, who are often left out of the conversation on what a just settlement looks like. JVP is home to thousands of Jews who reject or question Zionism and who support boycotting companies that maintain links with Israel's occupation and settlement building. Many JVP members are young people deeply committed to their religious tradition and disgusted by how Zionism has co-opted and captured many Jewish spaces. JVP, along with groups like American Muslims for Palestine, signifies how religiously inspired activism is a core part of the US movement for justice in the region. During the Gaza assault, membership in Jewish Voice for Peace surged, with new chapters sprouting up and donations pouring in.

A second group that signaled the change in discourse among American Jews was If Not Now, which was created as the assault on Gaza carried on. Many of the founders of the group, which takes its name from a famous quote by the Jewish sage Hillel, were active in J Street, the liberal Zionist lobby group, while in college. During the Gaza attack, however, they did not follow J Street's lead by supporting Israel's "right to defend its citizens." Instead, If Not Now, a grassroots group of young Jews, threw themselves into passionate activism that challenged the sclerotic self-appointed leaders of the Jewish community. They held Shabbat services in New York City's Washington Square Park while reciting the names of the most recent Palestinians and Israelis to perish during Israel's Gaza attack. And they protested outside the offices of the Conference of Presidents of Major American Jewish Organizations, calling on the Jewish establishment to press for an end to the occupation of Palestinian lands.

"You have more people who have only seen Israel as an occupying state and are standing up now," twenty-seven-year-old Kara Segal, an If Not Now organizer, told me. The polls back Segal up. As Israeli bombs rained down on Gaza, the respected polling center Gallup released data that showed how four decades of occupation have eroded Israel's image in the eyes of the American public. Only 36 percent of those between the ages of thirty and forty-nine said Israel's military actions were justified. The number dropped to 25 percent among eighteen- to twenty-nine-year-olds. In October 2013, the Pew Research Center, another polling outfit, released what it called a "portrait of Jewish Americans." After interviewing 3,500 Jews in every state, the Pew numbers showed that 26 percent of young Jews (ages eighteen to twenty-nine) thought the Israeli government was sincere about peace, compared to 43 percent of those over fifty.

To non-Jewish Americans, the numbers may seem strange. Jews are thought to be supportive of the Israeli government, a stereotype fueled by the American Jewish establishment and Israeli leaders' claims that Jews worldwide are part of Israel and that Prime Minister Benjamin Netanyahu is the leader of all Jews.

The idea that Jews are inextricably linked to Israel is relatively new, though. Hillel is a case in point. As the *New Republic*'s John Judis wrote in January 2014, Harvard Hillel declared in 1944 that it was "neither Zionist nor anti-Zionist." While that phrase is a radical departure from Hillel's current policy, it was mild when compared to other American Jewish leaders at the time, many of whom utterly rejected Zionism's ethos that Jews were a nation and needed a nation-state. It was common for Reform Jewish leaders in the nineteenth and twentieth centuries to say things like, "America is my national home," as Rabbi David Phillipson, a leading Reform figure most famous for his work in Cincinnati, Ohio, told Congress during a hearing on Zionism in 1922. In 1957, the sociologist Nathan Glazer surveyed American Jews and determined that Israel "had remarkably slight effects on the inner life of American Jewry."

However, Jewish views have drastically changed in the years since 1967, when Israel captured Jerusalem, the West Bank, Gaza, the Sinai and the Golan Heights from Arab states in the Six-Day War. American Jewish leaders moved firmly into the Zionist camp, and have stayed there since. This move coincided with the larger American establishment's embrace of Israel as a natural ally against the Soviet Union and the Arab states the Soviets supported. In his book *Knowing Too Much: Why the American Jewish Romance With Israel Is Coming to an End*, the scholar Norman Finkelstein argues that Israel's victory "facilitated the assimilation of American Jews." (Finkelstein notes this was "paradoxical" since Zionism's ethos is that Jews are alien in non-Jewish societies.) Israel's 1967 victory, then, was not only a point of pride for American Jews, who did see Israel as a plucky little democracy battling Arab savages. The victory was also crucial to US hegemony in the region, a reality that made American Jews all the more eager to support the state since it made their assimilation into the ruling establishment easier.

The result of America's unremitting support for the state of Israel is that the country has acted with impunity in its dealings with the Palestinians. Carried out with American weapons paid for by American tax dollars, Israel's brutality in Gaza, the West Bank, and Jerusalem has increased with barely a peep from US officials. And every single war in Gaza has been fully supported by the American Jewish leadership. That blind support is not being replicated at the grassroots level, however. Segments of the American Jewish community are returning to the sentiments voiced by Phillipson, although these Jews couch their opposition to Israel with sympathy for Palestinians, the primary victims of Israeli policy. Rabbi Phillipson's testimony to Congress in 1922 did not mention how the Zionist project would harm the rights of Palestinian Arabs. They were, it seems, invisible to Phillipson. But today, the Palestinian plight, broadcast by modern media, is the central reason why Israel is losing support. Israel's occupation is breeding resentment among young Jews. Increasing racism in Israel, combined with no end in sight to settlements, extrajudicial assassinations, and bombings of Gaza, is a petri dish for disaffection with Israel. Increasing numbers of academic groups and cultural figures are supporting the Boycott, Divestment and Sanctions movement. Many of those new voices belong to Jews.

The collapse of the pro-Israel consensus among American Jews will not bring about an end to the occupation. It will, however, be an important dent in the armor of America's Israel policy, which is also held up by Christian Zionists, the arms industry that profits from Israeli and American warfare, and American interest in hegemony in the Middle East.

A changed Jewish community is not the endgame, but it is a starting point. It will take away an ideological weapon that boosts US support for Israel. If Jewish support for Israel collapses, the charge of anti-Semitism leveled at critics of the state will lose its impact. Liberal politics, an arena where many American Jews are active, may also be transformed into a place where Israel criticism is commonplace. Jewish support for Israel cannot be taken for granted much longer. The floodgates of dissent are bursting—and the American Jewish community, bound up with supporting Israel for so long, will be changed forever.

What Is Anti-Semitism Now?

Sarah Schulman

The effort to differentiate between Jews and Israel is both historically accurate, and a ploy. On the one hand, there have always been Jews who opposed a nation-state. For some, it is the concept of nationalism itself that they reject. Some very religious Jews believe that it is only the Messiah who can redeem the diaspora. Communists center their hopes on the maintenance of that same diasporic existence. *If only we could all be internationalists, identifying across national borders, then* . . . And there have been mainstream integrated and assimilated Jews who have questioned, opposed, proposed reconfigurations of the Jewish state in Israel *because* of the Palestinians' rights being recognized as inherent. From Hannah Arendt to Noam Chomsky to Judith Butler, legitimized voices have dissented from the actual application of Zionism as it is imposed on that specific space. So, given these historic realities, the separation of Israel and "the Jews" has a legitimate experiential base.

At the same time, much of World Jewry, on the whole, has stood by, in either active or passive support, and allowed Israel to speak for us. Through occupation, apartheid, dehumanization, mass incarceration, violence, and genocide, we have not reacted. And I am ashamed to say that I include myself in this category, since I did not wake up and take responsibility until as late as 2009. We have mis-understood, ignored, indulged sentimentalism, applied ahistorical principles, capitulated to every dangerous lure of familial "loyalty" and felt afraid, held racist beliefs, and embraced supremacy ideology. We have planted trees, folk danced, celebrated holidays without questioning their veracity and/or have remained indifferent, dissociated and immune. So, Israel could not have devolved to this base condition without the nod or hand-up or indifference of World Jewry. Increasingly we are repulsed, and yet it would be dishonest to claim this as anyone's monster but our own.

Redemption is crucial to Judaism. It's what "we" are all seeking and is the central image of our collective struggle. And so we now have the benefit of the handful of enlightened among us who fought Zionism and Jewish supremacy when it was dangerous, impossible, and highly stigmatizing. I thank them personally for giving me a way out. And I am grateful today for the fruits of their labor, including organizations like Jewish Voice for Peace, which of this writing has 190,000 supporters and sixty chapters across the United States. These dissenters and the fruits of their just opposition hold the key to any possible rescue of Judaism from the abyss of the Israeli failure.

So, when we ask "What is anti-Semitism?" the first definition that usually arises is: "holding sweeping unilateral views of an entire people." And yes, those concepts are alive and energetic. The American Jew is seen as rich, stingy, smart, duplicitous, and the Israeli version as brutal, racist, violent. Add to both categories: self-righteous and entitled. And while I recognize some of these attributes in some people I know and in myself, I also see the contradictions, complexities, exceptions, and rejections. The second most common definition of anti-Semitism is: "holding all Jews responsible for the actions of some." This is both true and untrue. Yes, Jews are imagined as a group: and anything that rejects individuation is untrue. Israel could not have existed, or become the disaster that it is, if only the Jews wanted it to be that way. Military interests, Christian Zionism, and the desire to not assimilate millions of sick, traumatized refugees are all forces converging on the creation of this event. But on the other hand, World Jewry is, in many ways, responsible for what is happening in Israel, because we stood by at crucial moments and haven't stopped the injustice, although more and more of us are trying.

Then there is political anti-Semitism as manifested by rising fascist movements around the world, as Judith Butler pointed out in her talk at the Open Hillel Conference at Harvard in fall 2014. Golden Dawn, the Greek fascist party, now has elected representatives in the parliament. Hungary's neo-Nazi Jobbik party received 21 percent of the vote in that country's last election. Of course, American Christian Zionists, while supporting Israel, are traditional fundamentalists who believe that Jews returning to the Holy Land is a necessary part of the end times in which born-again Christians will escape death as they are raptured into heaven. And traditionally anti-Semitic movements like France's National Front also support Israel, while gaining their power base from Christian supremacist, anti-Muslim voters. So there is real anti-Semitism, some of which supports the Israeli state, and some of which does not.

Now, we have the "new anti-Semitism," where Jewish intellectuals and renegades who side with Palestinians and oppose occupation are called "anti-Semites." It's a badge of honor, frankly, and one I am proud to have been branded with. It comes from the Israeli government's propaganda machine, from the rightwing Jewish press, and from leaders of the organizations and movements that support current Israeli government policy. I have heard a number of explanations for this kind of attack. Naomi Brussel of Queers Against Israeli Apartheid, New York, speaking at the Homonationalism and Pinkwashing Conference at CUNY in April 2012, said, "These are people who honestly believe that if the Occupation ends they are going to the gas chamber tomorrow." I recognize this representation of paranoia as authentic. Butler, speaking at Open Hillel, suggested that they "really know" that we are not anti-Semites, but they also know that that the accusation will hurt us and so they use it to hurt us. I also recognize this tactic, making false accusations—not because the accuser thinks or cares that they are true, but simply to wound and injure. But having been on the receiving end of a number of these myself, I would add that there is an element of mental illness involved. There is a distorted thinking, a distorted logic system that produces a dehumanizing inability to consider oppositional thinking with nuance or reason. And this comes somewhat from a combination of traumatized behavior and supremacy ideology, which often resemble each other, and produce each other.

However, in the meantime, we live in an era in which the government of Israel publicly proclaims itself "the leader of the World's Jews" and "the Jewish State." Tanks and planes that murdered 2,000 civilians in Gaza have Jewish stars painted on them. The Al-Aqsa Mosque is being threatened by Jewish fundamentalists, and Jewish Israeli soldiers and police scapegoat, bully, brutalize, falsely arrest, and murder Palestinians everyday, as Jews. In those contexts it is reasonable for an assaulted Palestinian or someone who supports them to agree that these actors are in fact who they say they are . . . "the Jews." For that reason, we must acknowledge that to respond by saying "Down with the Jews," or "Kill the Jews as they are killing us," or "Fight the Jews," is something other than anti-Semitism. Rather than blind, generalized prejudice, this is instead a recognition and mirroring of who they are being told their tormentors are. This is, in fact, resistance.

As difficult, tragic, repulsive, and devastating as the cruelty of the Israelis, their Jewish supporters, and bystanders is, it forces us to new levels of self confrontation that are awful, and yet necessary. There is a terrible grief involved in giving up concepts of Jewish exceptionalism. Not having a state means not having the responsibilities of a state. Not having a supremacy-based state apparatus means being free to imagine outside of the prison of nationalism. Living in diaspora with histories of pain and oppression has produced a sense of righteousness that we must discard. For many of us who are not religious, this reckoning is particularly wrenching because, since we don't have God, if we give up some inspiration that we may have taken from Jewishness, what do we have left? There is a lot of talk among the secular pro-Palestinian Jewish community that relies on the only thing we have left, a concept of

"Jewish values." It is true that of the many diverse and contradictory traditions within Judaism—both religious and secular—one of those is a tradition of people who commit to social justice from a place of Jewish values. Yet, if we define "Jewish values" by the beliefs and investments of the broad category of the Jewish people, we would have to include genocide and the murder of civilians as among contemporary "Jewish values." Every religion provides frameworks that can be and are used to create negotiation and reconciliation, or cruelty and division. Well, that is our problem. Judaism isn't ending, and when the occupation does end, as it will, how we will reconvene and re-understand ourselves remains to be seen. The redemption is deferred.

Reflection on the Israeli Army Shutting Down the Palestine Festival of Literature in the Month of May in 2009: Burning Books, a Bebelplatz in Jerusalem

Kevin Coval

Where they burn books, they will, in the end, burn human beings too.
Heinrich Heine

jews love books.
we dress them up
in crowns and gold
breast plates. fine
paper, our finest
calligraphy. our books
live in an ark lit by a flame
that always burns, a metaphor
for a G-d, we don't have
vowels for.

if we carry nothing
else into Diaspora, we carry

these stories, these scrolls
that unroll a history we revere
and parade thru aisles
on the highest of holy days.
we kiss the corner of tallis
to our lips, put cloth to text
to praise words Moses brought
off the mount, our ancestors
lugged thru the desert. stories
told and told again at a kitchen
table somewhere, the 5th and 15th
time we heard them bored out
our seder mind, but the 50th
and 502nd time something stuck
so we wrote them down
in our most reverent hand style
in the blackest of ink on bone
parchment. we record the trials
and rivals and lineage and heroes
of our families cuz we love books
mourn all the storied bodies
burned by the those who hate books
with messy endings. we love books
cuz books are bodies of stories
and stories make history
and we are a people who believe
in the stories of people to tell history
and mourn all the bodies and stories
burned before they are recorded
in the Eternal book, authored
by the voiceless and Voweless.

but it is 2009/5769

& this spring Israeli troops shut down The Palestine Festival of Literature
behind barrels of guns. they stormed into a theater where poets were
reading poems
& demanded silence behind triggers where bullets scream & governments
check point
& knessets approve military bombardments & schools bombed & burned
on ground they are meant to be on fire from words & ideas, not metal.

in the name of a jewish state
Israeli educated young men aimed guns in the faces of women
reading poems. in the name of a jewish state stories silence forever.

which raises the question(s):
who are we because of empire? what democracy are we scared of?
how can we deny the right to sing, to chazzan a Palestinian song?

mad men bring books to the bond fire.
power mad men bring bodies.

our books been banned & burned & bordered, bodied into boxes
& camps cuz they demand memory, insist our presence in the story
of the world & books are memory of never forgetting & people house books
in their stories & stories should never be crushed by missiles. books record
the day
& days in exile & days that should not have been recorded. the horrors &
the horrible. the record of families spilt & broken & bastards forever. books
are records that never forget & preserve & serve memory & history when
militarized revisers deny events
as lived by the natives. the records prove otherwise, proof of existence &
empires
want proof of purchase & per chance & pursue silencing stories that make
them look criminal in the honest of day & moon of night.

records are stories, a people
hold dear. who knows this
more than us?

> all us   wandering immigrants
> all us   seekers of safe land
> all us   unfettered poets of wind
> all us   literate builders of pidgins
> all us   inventors with scraps
> all us   people of the book

though we don't seem to know much
anymore   except the havoc
reaped on our bodies in exile, the learned
behavior of executioners we internalize
the bureaucracies & boots & lines of refugees
we terrorize. gather families into open air
prisons & worse. we bury bodies in graves
of steel. bodies who house forests of stories.
where is the ark in the center of the congregation
the ark in the center of the city of peace filled
with bodies of stories, records stacked and unfurled
unsequestered & unsilenced.

it is mad men who burn books
& bodies & hold poets at gun point

this the work of emperors & empires
furors & fascists. scared colonists
insane to control what no state could
the record of people living
despite the state's efforts
to have them not.

Endnotes

A Gaza Breviary

1 Michael Tracey on Twitter at https://twitter.com/mtracey/status/492830719119355904.

2 "Jadaliyya Co-Editor Noura Erakat Debates the Tactics and Ethics of Warfare on PBS Newshour," at jadaliyya.com.

3 "Hamas Shows Resilience in Face of Israeli Ground Incursion," *Washington Post*, July 19, 2014, at washingtonpost.com.

4 Interviewer: "We have heard that a half million children have died [because of the sanctions imposed by the United States on Iraq]. I mean, that's more children than died in Hiroshima. And, you know, is the price worth it?" Madeline Albright: "I think this is a very hard choice, but the price—we think the price is worth it" (*60 Minutes*, May 12, 1996).

5 Madeline Albright: "But the bottom line is, I think, that this is hurting Israel's moral authority. I do think that it looks as though they are overdoing it" (CNN, July 23, 2014).

6 "Don't Cut Off Debate With Israeli Institutions—Enrich It Instead," *Chronicle of Higher Education*, December 31, 2013, at chronicle.com.

7   "Israeli Universities Lend Support to Gaza Massacre," July 25, 2014, at electronicinti-
    fada.net.

8   "We Are Israeli Reservists. We Refuse to Serve," *Washington Post*, July 23, 2014, at
    washingtonpost.com.

9   James Baldwin, "Open Letter to the Born Again," *Nation*, September 29, 1978, at
    thenation.com.

10 Ruth R. Wisse, "Israel and the Intellectuals: A Failure of Nerve?" *Commentary
    Magazine*, May 1, 1988, at commentarymagazine.com.

11 "9 Jewish Activists Arrested After Occupying Friends of the Israel Defense Forces
    Office," July 22, 2014, at mondoweiss.net.

12 ImadMesdoua on Twitter at https://twitter.com/ImadMesdoua/status/4913002722880
    47104.

13 "Hamas Wants to Pile Up 'Telegenically-Dead Palestinians for Their Cause' —
    Netanyahu, on Television," July 20, 2014, at mondoweiss.net.

14 Nicholas Kristof, "Who's Right and Wrong in the Middle East," *New York Times*, July
    20, 2014, at nytimes.com.

15 "US Academic Group Votes to Boycott Israeli Universities," *Washington Post*,
    December 16, 2013, at washingtonpost.com.

16 Allison Kaplan Sommer, "Routine Emergencies," *Haaretz*, July 21, 2014, at
    haaretz.com.

17 Selena Gomez, Jon Stewart, Rob Schneider, Rosie O'Donnell, Mark Ruffalo, John
    Cusack, Anthony Bourdain. See "8 Surprising Celebrities Outraged by Israel's Assault
    Gaza," July 23, 2014, at alternet.org.

18 "Rihanna, I Didn't Even Realize I Tweeted #Free Palestine," July 15, 2014, at
    tmz.com.

19 "Senate Unanimously Passes Resolution Supporting Israel," July 18, 2014, at
    mondoweiss.net.

20 "Senate Passes Resolution in Support of Israel," July 17, 2014, at thehill.com.

21 "Don't Cut Off Debate With Israeli Institutions — Enrich It Instead," *Chronicle of
    Higher Education*, December 31, 2013, at chronicle.com.

22 The New Republic on Twitter at https://twitter.com/tnr/status/490119313475776512.

23 Alex Kane on Twitter at https://twitter.com/alexbkane/status/490118682186878976.

24 David Frum on Twitter at https://twitter.com/davidfrum/status/488778742106308609.

25 "A Handful of Israeli Academics Responds to Calls to Condemn Gaza Slaughter," July 14, 2014, at electronicintifada.net.

26 "Don't Cut Off Debate With Israeli Institutions—Enrich It Instead," *Chronicle of Higher Education*, December 31, 2013, at chronicle.com.

27 Steven Erlanger, "In Gaza Airstrikes and Economic Stress Make for an Anxious Ramadan," *New York Times*, July 11, 2014, at nytimes.com.

28 Gideon Levy, "Our Wretched Jewish State," *Haaretz*, July 6, 2014, at haaretz.com.

Yes, I Said, "National Liberation"

1 See Walter Rodney, *How Europe Underdeveloped Africa*, Howard University Press, 1981, (orig. 1972); Cedric Robinson, *Black Marxism: The Making of the Black Radical Tradition*, Zed Books, 1983; Chinweizu, *The West and the Rest of Us: White Predators, Black Enslavers, and the African Elite*, Random House, 1975; Angela Davis, *Women, Race and Class*, Random House, 1981; Vincent Harding, *There Is a River: The Black Struggle for Freedom in America*, Random House, 1983; Manning Marable, *Blackwater: Historical Studies in Race, Class Consciousness and Revolution*, Black Praxis Press, 1981, and *How Capitalism Underdeveloped Black America*, South End Press, 1982; Cornel West, *Prophesy Deliverance: An Afro-American Revolutionary Christianity*, Westminister, 1982; Barbara Smith's many articles, some of which were later collected in *The Truth That Never Hurts: Writings on Race, Gender and Freedom*, Rutgers University Press, 1998; and the essential edited collections, Barbara Smith, Gloria T. Hull, and Patricia Bell Scott, eds., *All the Women Are White, All the Blacks Are Men, But Some of Us Are Brave: Black Women's Studies*, The Feminist Press, 1982; *Home Girls: A Black Feminist Anthology*, Women of Color Press, 1983; Edward Said, *Orientalism*, Pantheon, 1978, and *The Question of Palestine*, Vintage, 1980. We read Eqbal Ahmad's essays in *Monthly Review*, *Nation*, and related publications, recently collected in *The Selected Writings of Eqbal Ahmad*, eds. Carollee Bengelsdorf, Margaret Cerullo, and Yogesh Chandrani, Columbia University Press, 2006. Among Samir Amin's many books, most influential at the time was *Unequal Development: An Essay on the Social Formations of Peripheral Capitalism*, Monthly Review Press, 1976. For a deeper examination of Third World/national liberation movements and the place of Palestine, see Vijay Prashad, *The Darker Nations: A People's History of the*

Third World, New Press, 2007; Paul Thomas Chamberlin, *The Global Offensive: The United States, the Palestine Liberation Organization, and the Making of the Post–Cold War Order*, Oxford University Press, 2012.

2 Yousef Munayyer, "How BDS Is Educating the Public About Israel's Brutal Policies," *Nation*, July 10, 2014; and Noam Chomsky, "On Israel-Palestine and BDS," *Nation*, July 2, 2014. See also the excellent response to Chomsky from the Organizing Collective of the US Campaign for the Academic and Cultural Boycott of Israel, "How BDS Has Galvanized the Struggle for Justice in Palestine," *Nation*, July 10, 2014.

3 Jaime Omar Yassin, "The Shortest Distance Between Ferguson and Palestine," *Counterpunch*, August 15–17, 2014; Dean Obeidallah, "Michael Brown, Gaza, and Muslim Americans," *Daily Beast*, August 20, 2014; Sydney Levy, "Jewish Voice for Peace Stands in Solidarity With the Community of Ferguson, Missouri," August 20, 2014, at jewishvoiceforpeace.org; David Gilbert, "Michael Brown Shooting: Gaza Strip Tweets Ferguson About How to Deal With Tear Gas," *International Business Times*, August 14, 2014. For an excellent critique of the tendency to attribute militarized policing to Israeli training without considering America's long history of militarized law enforcement, see Mark LeVine, "Ferguson Is Not Gaza . . . Yet," *Al Jazeera America*, August 18, 2014.

4 Joseph Schapiro, "In Ferguson, Court Fines and Fees Fuel Anger," August 25, 2014, at npr.org.

5 Similar statistics can be replicated across the country. Five times as many whites use illegal drugs as African Americans, and yet black people are sent to prison on drug charges at ten times the rate of whites. See the Criminal Justice Fact Sheet at naacp.org.

6 See the excellent essay by Maya Mikdashi, "Can Palestinian Men Be Victims?" *Jadaliyya*, July 23, 2014, at jadaliyya.com.

7 Sedef Arat-Koç, "Human Rights Discourse Fails Palestinian Quest for Justice," *Rabble News*, February 2, 2009, at rabble.ca.

8 Ahdaf Soueif, "Dead Palestinian Children in Gaza Tell Story of Impunity," July 31, 2014, at latimes.com.

9 Nathan Guttman, "Christian Backers of Israel Reach Out to Blacks," October 19, 2011, at forward.com; Ira Glunts, "The Pro-Israel Lobby Courts African Americans," November 6, 2011, at truth-out.org.

10 Eddie Glaude, *Exodus!: Religion, Race and Nation in Early Nineteenth-Century Black America*, University of Chicago Press, 2000; Keith P. Feldman, "Representing Permanent War: Black Power's Palestine and the End(s) of Civil Rights," *New Centennial Review*, 8:2 (Fall 2008), 199. There is a very long history of Black Zionism beyond the scope of this short essay. Just on Marcus Garvey's Zionist leanings and influences, see for example, Robert A. Hill and Barbara Bair, eds., *Marcus Garvey: Life and Lessons*, University of California Press, 1987, lv–lvi; see also Jacob S. Dorfman, *Black Israelites: The Rise of American Black Israelite Religions*, Oxford University Press, 2014, 113–34; Shana L. Redmond, *Anthem: Social Movements and the Sound of Solidarity in the African Diaspora*, New York University Press, 2014, 32–4.

11 "Randolph Urges Negro Support Palestine Jews," *Amsterdam News*, March 6, 1948. W. E. B. Du Bois had long championed a Jewish state and took no heed in Ralph Bunche's failed efforts to promote a binational alternative to partition. Several years before Israel's founding, Du Bois lamented, "The only thing that has stopped the extraordinary expansion of the Jews in Palestine has been the Arab population and the attempt on the part of English and Arabs to keep Palestine from becoming a complete Jewish state." Quoted in Alex Lubin, *Geographies of Liberation: The Making of an Afro-Arab Political Imaginary*, University of North Carolina Press, 2014, 105. See also, DuBois, "The Winds of Time," *Chicago Defender*, May 15, 1948; and Du Bois, "The Case for the Jews," *Chicago Star*, May 8, 1948; see also Melani McAlister, *Epic Encounters: Culture, Media, and US Interests in the Middle East Since 1945*, University of California Press, 2005, 89.

12 *Atlanta Daily World*, March 3, 1948. See also Charles A. Davis, "Palestine Educator Seeks Model for Jewish Schools," *Chicago Defender*, May 15, 1948.

13 George S. Schuyler, "Views and Reviews," *Pittsburgh Courier*, June 19, 1948. This was not Schuyler's only column on Palestine. See "Views and Reviews," *Pittsburgh Courier*, March 27, 1948. *Courier* columnist P. L. Prattis held a diametrically opposing view. He compared Israel's fight for independence with African colonies under British rule, and excoriated the Truman administration for balking on its support for partition. Prattis, "The Horizon," *Pittsburgh Courier*, April 3, 1948. Another Black critic of Israel's treatment of the Arabs was Robert Durr, "Speaking Out," *Chicago Defender*, July 10, 1948.

14 "What You Buy With Blood," *Pittsburgh Courier*, July 17, 1948.

15 Amy Kaplan's excellent essay, "Zionism as Anticolonialism: The Case of *Exodus*," *American Literary History*, 25:4 (Winter 2013), 870–95, makes a similar point about how Leon Uris's novel, *Exodus*, and the subsequent Hollywood interpretation of the book, produced a narrative of Israel's founding as an anticolonial struggle against British domination.

16 Keith P. Feldman adds yet another layer to this argument by revealing how postwar racial liberalism and the promise of an integrated democracy undermined a radical critique of Israel's emerging racial/colonial order. Israel was represented as a modern, integrated democracy along US lines, and the ideology of racial liberalism erased historical and contemporary racial violence. Feldman, "Representing Permanent War," 200–1. See also Feldman's brilliant forthcoming book, *A Shadow Over Palestine: The Imperial Life of Race in America*, University of Minnesota Press, 2015.

17 Quoted in Uri Davis, *Apartheid Israel: Possibilities for the Struggle Within*, Zed Books, 2003, 87.

18 Quoted in Sasha Polakow-Suransky, *The Unspoken Alliance: Israel's Secret Relationship With Apartheid South Africa*, Random House, 2010, 5.

19 Melani McAlister, "One Black Allah: The Middle East in the Cultural Politics of African American Liberation, 1955–1970," *American Quarterly*, 51:3 (September 1999), 622–56; and Prashad, *The Darker Nations*, 51–2, 99–100.

20 Benny Morris, *Righteous Victims: A History of the Zionist-Arab Conflict, 1881–1998*, Vintage Books, 2001, 275.

21 "Zionist Logic," *Egyptian Gazette*, September 17, 1964. See also Sohail Daulatzai, *Black Star, Crescent Moon: The Muslim International and Black Freedom Beyond America*, University of Minnesota Press, 2012, 40–5.

22 See Lubin, *Geographies of Liberation*, 119–30.

23 Student Nonviolent Coordinating Committee, "Third World Round-up: The Palestine Problem: Test Your Knowledge," *SNCC Newsletter* 1.2 (July–August 1967), 5–6. Feldman, "Representing Permanent War," 210–1, provides the best discussion of the SNCC essay. See also Lubin's excellent treatment in *Geographies of Liberation*, 117–19.

24 The published interview appeared in "Conversation With Martin Luther King," *Conservative Judaism*, 22:3 (Spring 1968), 1–19.

25 "Conversation With Martin Luther King," 11.

26 Ibid., 12.

27 Ibid., 12.

28 King's speech "Beyond Vietnam: A Time to Break Silence," delivered April 4, 1967, can be found all over the Internet and has been reprinted in numerous published collections.

This Is Not The University of Michigan Anymore

1 For more on the destruction of Palestinian towns and villages in the lead-up to the establishment of the state of Israel, *see* Pappe Ilan, *The Ethnic Cleansing of Palestine* (2nd Ed.), London: Oneworld Publications, 2007.

2 From September 16–18, 1982, the Israeli military, led by Defense Minister Ariel Sharon, surrounded the Sabra and Shatila Palestinian refugee camps in Lebanon, while Lebanese Phalangist Militia went in and massacred civilians. See Robert Fist, "The Legacy of Ariel Sharon—The Butcher of Sabra and Chatila," *Independent* (Manchester), February 6, 2001, available at: rense.com, (accessed January 25, 2013). A UN commission as well as an Israeli commission set up to investigate both found that Ariel Sharon bore responsibility for the attack. See Seán MacBride, et al., *Israel in Lebanon: The Report of International Commission to enquire into reported violations of International Law by Israel during its invasion of the Lebanon*, (London: Ithaca Press, 1983), 191–2, and Kahan Commission, *Report of the Commission of Inquiry Into the Events at the Refugee Camps in Beirut*, February 8,1983, available at: fr.org, (accessed December 3, 2014).

3 Likud spokesman Ofir Akounis quoted in CNN, "Palestinians say opposition tour of holy site could cause bloodshed," September 27, 2000, available in part at: journals. democraticunderground.com (accessed December 3, 2014).

4 B'Tselem, *Statistics: Fatalities Before Operation Cast Lead*, at btselem.org; see also "Time Line of Second (Al-Aqsa) Intifada," MidEast Web, available at mideastweb.org, (accessed November 19, 2014).

5 See e.g., Amira Hass, "Interview With a Sharpshooter," *Haaretz*, November 20, 2000, available at: labournet.net, (accessed November 19, 2014); Reuven Pedatzur, "More Than a Million Bullets," *Haaretz*, June 29, 2004, athaaretz.com (accessed November 19, 2014).

6 For more about the history of Palestinian popular struggle against the Israeli

occupation, see Mazin Qumsiyeh, *Popular Resistance in Palestine: A History of Hope and Empowerment* (London: Pluto Press, 2010). See also Peter Ackerman and Jack DuVall, "The Intifada: Campaign for a Homeland," in *A Force More Powerful* (New York: St. Martin's Press, 2000).

7   In May 2000, Israeli forces ended the occupation of southern Lebanon following a sustained guerrilla campaign led by Hezbollah. This was largely seen as vindication for those who would argue that Israel would only yield to force.

8   See Iain Scobbie, "Is Gaza Still Occupied Territory?" *Forced Migration Review 26,* (2006): 18, available at fmreview.org (accessed January 23, 2013), in which he reviews the test employed by international law to determine whether territory is occupied, and determines that according to international standards, Gaza remains occupied. For more comprehensive law and analysis on the topic of the beginning and end of occupation, see International Committee of the Red Cross (ICRC), Expert Meeting Report: *Occupation and Other Forms of Administration of Foreign Territory*, March 2012, icrc.org (accessed January 25, 2013).

9   There are five land crossings between Gaza and Israel, all of which are controlled by Israel. The only other land crossing with Gaza is to Egypt. This crossing, Rafah, is indirectly controlled by Israel by way of Israeli-Egyptian understandings. Palestinians with Palestinian ID cards are forbidden to use the Israeli airports and are forced to travel via land to Jordan or Egypt to use an airport.

10   See Gisha, *Two Years of Gaza Closures by the Numbers*, at gisha.org (accessed December 3, 2014).

11   Gisha, *Restrictions on the Transfer of Goods to Gaza: Obstruction and Obfuscation*, January 2010, note 2, quoting a January 13, 2010, letter from the Coordinator of Government Activities in the Territories (COGAT) to Gisha, at gisha.org (accessed December 3, 2014).

12   Save the Children and Medical Aid for Palestinians, *Gaza's Children: Falling Behind, The Effect of the Blockade on Child Health in Gaza*, 2012 Report at savethechildren. org.uk (accessed December 3, 2014).

13   For news reports of this action, see "Palestinian 'Freedom Riders' Board Settlers' Bus," BBC News, November 15, 2011; Collard, Rebecca, "Palestinian 'freedom Riders' board Israeli buses in protest," *Christian Science Monitor*, November 15, 2011, at csmonitor. com; Horowitz, Adam, "Six Palestinian Freedom Riders Arrested Traveling on Israeli-only Bus," *Mondoweiss*, November 15, 2011, at mondoweiss.net; Nour, Joudah. "From

US South to Palestine, Freedom Rides Change History," *Electronic Intifada*, November 16, 2011, at electronicintifada.net.

Samidoon: We Are Steadfast

1   Jillian Kestler-D'Amours, "Israel Arrests 'Freedom Riders' Challenging Apartheid Road System," *Electronic Intifada*, November 15, 2011.

2   Palestinian Freedom Riders, "Palestinian Freedom Riders to Ride Settler Buses to Jerusalem," PalFreedomRides.blogspot.com, November 13, 2011.

3   Angela Davis, "Angela Davis Endorses Palestinian Freedom Rides," PalFreedomRides. blogspot.com, November 14, 2011.

4   Nour Joudah, "From US South to Palestine, Freedom Rides Change History," *Electronic Intifada*, November 16, 2011.

5   Nora Barrows-Friedman, "Palestine Solidarity Activists Protest US Deportation Policies in Arizona," *Electronic Intifada*, October 11, 2013.

6   David Nakamura, "Frustration With White House Mounts for Immigration Advocates," *Washington Post*, September 18, 2013.

7   Barrows-Friedman, "Palestine Solidarity Activists Protest US Deportation Policies in Arizona."

8   Jimmy Johnson, "Contractor for Israel's Apartheid Wall Wins US Border Contract," *Electronic Intifada*, March 1, 2014.

9   Land Day is marked every year with tremendous marches by Palestinians inside Israel, the West Bank, Gaza, Lebanon, and Syria, demanding the right to return to their homeland and an end to Israeli colonization.

10   Mizrahim are Jewish peoples of Arab, Middle Eastern, and North African descent. Many Mizrahim speak Arabic and other languages of North Africa and western Asia. Mizrahi Jews living in present-day Israel experience prejudice and racism from Ashkenazim (Jews of European descent).

11   Rania Khalek and Adriana Maestas, "How the Israel Lobby Is Courting US Latinos," *Electronic Intifada*, February 27, 2014.

12   Khalek and Maestas, "How the Israel Lobby Is Courting US Latinos." The quote is from Michael Freund, "Fundamentally Freund: Time for Hispanic 'Hasbara,'" *Jerusalem Post*, November 14, 2012.

13   Ali Abunimah, *The Battle for Justice in Palestine*, Chicago: Haymarket, 2014, p. 212.

14 Belen Fernandez, "Israel's Other Silent War," *Al Jazeera English*, November 17, 2013.

15 Ali Abunimah, "Israeli Lawmaker Miri Regev: 'Heaven Forbid' We Compare Africans to Human Beings," *Electronic Intifada*, May 31, 2012.

16 Reuters, "Israel to Jail Illegal Migrants for up to Three Years," UK.Reuters.com, June 3, 2012.

17 Seth Freed Wessler, "The Israel Lobby Finds a New Face: Black College Students," *Colorlines*, January 18, 2012.

18 Ta-Nehisi Coates, "Trayvon Martin and the Irony of American Justice," *Atlantic*, July 15, 2013.

19 Students for Justice in Palestine, "Palestine Justice Groups Statement of Solidarity With Trayvon Martin & Victims of Racial Violence," SJPNational.org, August 14, 2013.

20 Judd Yadid, "10 Ways to Discover Israel's Miraculously Well-Endowed LGBT Scene," *Haaretz*, March 24, 2014.

21 Sarah Schulman, "Israel and 'Pinkwashing,'" *New York Times*, November 22, 2011, and *Israel/Palestine and the Queer International*, Durham: Duke University Press, 2012.

22 Ghaith Hilal, "Eight Questions Palestinian Queers Are Tired of Hearing," *Electronic Intifada*, November 27, 2013.

The US Boycott of Palestine

1 "US Aid to Israel Totals $234 Billion Since 1948," *Middle East Monitor*, March 22, 2013, at middleeastmonitor.com.

2 Stephen Zunes, "The Strategic Uses of US Aid to Israel," *Washington Report on Middle East Affairs*, at wrmea.org.

3 See, for example, Shir Hever, *The Political Economy of Israel's Occupation: Repression Beyond Exploitation*, Pluto Press, 2010.

4 Jethro Mullen and Ben Wedeman, 'They Went to the Beach to Play': Deaths of 4 Children Add to Growing Toll in Gaza Conflict," *CNN World*, July 17, 2014, at cnn. com.

5 Peter Hart, "New York Times Re-Writes Gaza Headline: Was It Too Accurate?," *FAIR: Fairness & Accuracy in Reporting*, July 17, 2014, at fair.org.

6 Ramsey Cox, "Senate Passes Resolution Supporting Israel," *Hill*, July 29, 2014, at thehill.com.

7 Ken Klippenstein and Paul Gottinger, "US Provides Israel the Weapons Used on Gaza," *Truthout*, July 23, 2014, at truth-out.org.

8 Peter Coy, "Why More of Israel's Iron Dome Will Be Made in the US," *Bloomberg Business Week*, July 16, 2014, at businessweek.com.

9 Quoted in Klippenstein and Gottinger, "US Provides Israel the Weapons Used on Gaza."

10 Edward Said, *The Question of Palestine*, Vintage Books, 1992 (1979), 231–2.

11 "Legal Consequences of the Construction of a Wall in the Occupied Palestinian Territory," International Court of Justice, Press Release 2004/28, July 9, 2014, at icj-cij. org.

12 Palestinian Civil Society Call for Boycott, at bdsmovement.net.

13 Ibid.

14 Ali Abunimah, *The Battle for Justice in Palestine*, Haymarket Books, 2014.

15 Right to Education Campaign, "Denial of Entry and Its Impact on Higher Education," *Electronic Intifada*, January 6, 2007, at electronicintifada.net.

16 "The Right to Education Campaign's Submission to the United Nations Human Rights Council's Universal Periodic Review of Israel December 2008 Submitted July 2008," at righttoenter.ps.

17 Alternative Information Center, "Academic Boycott of Israel and the Complicity of Israeli Academic Institutions in Occupation of Palestinian Territories," October 2009, at usacbi.files.wordpress.com.

18 George Lipsitz, *American Studies in a Moment of Danger*, University of Minnesota Press, 2001, xv–xvi.

About the Authors

Alex Kane is a freelance journalist whose work focuses on the American Jewish community, Israel/Palestine, US foreign policy, and civil liberties. A former editor at Mondoweiss and AlterNet, his work has appeared in the *Los Angeles Review of Books*, *VICE*, *Salon*, and more.

Alex Lubin is the chair of the American Studies Department at the University of New Mexico. From 2011–13, he served as the director of the Center for American Studies and Research at the American University of Beirut. His books include *Romance and Rights: The Politics of Interracial Intimacy, 1945–54* (2004) and *Geographies of Liberation: The Making of an Afro-Arab Political Imaginary* (2014). His edited books include *American Studies Between the American Century and the Arab Spring* (with Marwan Kriady) and *The Cultural Front in the US War on Terror* (with Lisa Hajjar).

Ben Ehrenreich is the author of two novels, *Ether* and *The Suitors*. His journalism and essays have appeared in *Harper's*, the *New York Times*

Magazine, the *London Review of Books*, and many other publications. He is currently working on a nonfiction book based on his reporting from the West Bank.

Colin Dayan, the Robert Penn Warren Professor in the Humanities and Professor of Law at Vanderbilt University, is the author of *Haiti, History and the Gods; The Story of Cruel and Unusual;* and *The Law Is a White Dog: How Legal Rituals Make and Unmake Persons.* Elected a fellow of the American Academy of Arts and Sciences in 2012, she also writes for the *Boston Review,* Al Jazeera America, the *London Review of Books,* and the *Los Angeles Review of Books.*

Corey Robin is a professor of political science at Brooklyn College and the CUNY Graduate Center. He is the author of *Fear: The History of a Political Idea* and *The Reactionary Mind: Conservatism from Edmund Burke to Sarah Palin.*

Deema K. Shehabi is the author of *Thirteen Departures from the Moon,* co-editor with Beau Beausoleil of *Al-Mutanabbi Street Starts Here,* and co-author with Marilyn Hacker of *Diaspo/Renga.*

Fady Joudah is a physician of internal medicine. His poetry and translations have received a Yale Series prize, a Griffin International prize, and a Guggenheim fellowship. *Alight* and *Textu* are his most recent poetry collections. He hails from Isdud, Palestine.

Hayan Charara is the author of three poetry books: *Something Sinister* (2016), *The Sadness of Others* (2006), and *The Alchemist's Diary* (2001). He also edited *Inclined to Speak: An Anthology of Contemporary Arab American Poetry* (2008).

Huwaida Arraf is the co-founder of the International Solidarity Movement.

Jasiri X is a hip-hop artist, activist, and founder of One Hood Media Academy, which teaches African American boys how to analyze and create media for themselves. Jasiri X signed a record deal with Wandering Worx Entertainment and released his debut album, *Ascension*, with acclaimed producer RLGN.

Junot Díaz is the author of the Pulitzer Prize–winning *The Brief Wondrous Life of Oscar Wao* (2007) and two short-story collections, *Drown* (1996) and *This Is How You Lose Her* (2012). He is the 2012 MacArthur Fellow.

Kevin Coval is a poet, a founder of Louder Than a Bomb: The Chicago Youth Poetry Festival, and artistic director of Young Chicago Authors. He is the editor of *The Breakbeat Poets: New American Poetry in the Age of Hip Hip* (2015).

Lena Khalaf Tuffaha is a poet. She translated the screenplay for Annemarie Jacir's 2011 film *When I Saw You*. She is the co-founder of the Institute for Middle East Understanding (IMEU). Her poems appear in the collection *Being Palestinian* (2015).

Mumia Abu-Jamal is a writer who has spent the past thirty years on Pennsylvania's death row and is now in the general population, having been wrongfully convicted and sentenced for the murder of Philadelphia Police Officer Daniel Faulkner. His most recent book is *Writings on the Wall: Selected Prison Writings of Mumia Abu-Jamal* (City Lights, 2015).

Najla Said is an actress and writer. Her memoir, *Looking for Palestine: Growing Up Confused in an Arab American Family* (based on her solo performance piece, *Palestine*, which ran Off-Broadway in 2010) was published by Riverhead, a division of Penguin. She lives in New York.

Naomi Shihab Nye is the author, most recently, of *The Turtle of Oman* (Greenwillow, 2014). Her father Aziz Shihab's last book, *Does the Land Remember Me?: A Memoir of Palestine*, is available in paperback from Syracuse University Press.

Nora Barrows-Friedman is an associate editor of the *Electronic Intifada* and the author of *In Our Power: US Students Organize for Justice in Palestine* (Just World Books, 2014). She has been a print journalist and radio broadcaster covering Palestine since 2003.

Noura Erakat is a human rights attorney and activist. She is an assistant professor at George Mason University. She has taught international human rights law in the Middle East at Georgetown University since Spring 2009. Noura is a co-editor of *Jadaliyya*.

Philip Metres is the author of *Sand Opera* (2015), *A Concordance of Leaves* (2013), and *To See the Earth* (2008). A two-time recipient of the NEA and the Arab American Book Award, he is professor of English at John Carroll University.

Randa Jarrar is the author of *A Map of Home*, which won the Hopwood Award and was named one of the best novels of 2008 by the *Barnes and Noble Review*. In 2010, she was named one of the most gifted writers of Arab origin under the age of forty. Her work has appeared in the *New York Times Magazine*, *Guernica*, *Ploughshares*, and many others.

Remi Kanazi is a poet and writer based in New York City. He is the editor of *Poets for Palestine* (Al Jisser Group, 2008) and the author of *Poetic Injustice: Writings on Resistance and Palestine* (RoR Publishing, 2011). He recently appeared in the Palestine Festival of Literature as well as Poetry International. He is an organizing committee member for the US Campaign for the Academic and Cultural Boycott of Israel. His forthcoming collection of poetry is *Before the Next Bomb Drops* (Haymarket, 2015).

Robin D. G. Kelley is the Distinguished Professor of History & Gary B. Nash Endowed Chair of United States History at UCLA. He is the author of many groundbreaking works, including *Thelonious Monk: The Life and Times of an American Original* (2009) and *Africa Speaks, America Answers: Modern Jazz in Revolutionary Times* (2012).

Rumzi Araj produced *Slingshot Hip Hop*, which was an official selection of the 2008 Sundance Film Festival. He has also produced *Planet of the Arabs*, an official selection of the 2005 Sundance Film Festival.

Sarah Schulman is the author of seventeen books including *Israel/Palestine and The Queer International* (Duke) and the forthcoming *Conflict Is Not Abuse: Overstating Harm, Community Responsibility and the Duty of Repair*. She is Distinguished Professor of the Humanities at the City University of New York, College of Staten Island.

Sinan Antoon is a poet, whose collections include *Mawshur Muballal bil-Hurub* (Cairo, 2003) and *Laylun Wahidun fi Kull al-Mudun* (Beirut/Baghdad: Dar al-Jamal, 2010). His novels include *I'jaam* (2003), *Wahdaha Shajarat al-Rumman* (Beirut: al-Mu'assassa al-'Arabiyya, 2010, and al-Jamal, 2013) and *Ya Maryam* (Beirut: Dar al-Jamal, 2012). His second novel, translated as *The Corpse Washer*, won the 2014 Arab American Book Award; his third novel was on the short list for the Arabic Booker. His translation of Darwish, *In the Presence of Absence*, won the 2012 National Translation Award.

Teju Cole is the author of *Open City* (2012) and *Every Day Is for the Thief* (2007). He is the Distinguished Writer in Residence at Bard College.

Vijay Prashad is the author of seventeen books, most recently *No Free Left: The Futures of Indian Communism* (LeftWord Books). He is the chief editor at LeftWord Books (Delhi) and teaches at Trinity College.